The 11 Karmic Spaces

The 11 Karmic Spaces

*Choosing freedom from the
patterns that bind you*

Ma Jaya Sati Bhagavati

Kashi Publishing
Sebastian, Florida

Published by
Kashi Publishing
11155 Roseland Road
Sebastian, Florida 32958

Edited by Sw. Mata Giri Perkins & Jaya Priya Timell
Copyedited by Jennifer Read Hawthorne
Cover Art by Deb Sakini Davis
Cover and Book Design by Laurie Douglas
Photograph of Ma Jaya by JPI Studios
Photograph of Neem Karoli Baba by Ram Giri Braun

Printed in the United States of America

Before you begin: The benefits attributed to the practices suggested in this
book come from the centuries-old yogic tradition. Results will vary with
individuals. Nothing in this book is to be construed as medical advice.
Please consult a physician before beginning any exercise program.

ISBN: 978-0-9838228-0-6

*To the one who taught me to teach, to love, and to breathe,
my Guruji Neem Karoli Baba, who is my life.*

Contents

Foreword

If the great German philosopher, Hegel, had known Ma Jaya, he would have gone into a shock of recognition. For Hegel wrote about world-historical individuals, those richly endowed people whose personal interests, sensibilities, and passions correspond to the needs and turnings of their times. Out in front or behind the scenes, they are the impresarios of change, the orchestrators of culture and consciousness. Sometimes they are weirdly prescient, deeply empathic, even co-creative with the minds and hearts of those to whom they minister. Such is the wildly innovative genius of Ma Jaya.

A Midwife of Souls, she is also a confidant of Spirit, the one to whom one turns when the going gets rough, or one needs a shake-up in one's life process. With Ma, there is no division between traditionally accepted divided and distinguished worlds. Seer and Sorceress, Sage and Soul-crafter, she lifts the veil so that all can see the hidden workings of the Life within us. And this she does with no-nonsense tough love chastened by a compassion that knows no limits. This book of her teachings is a glorious testament to her psychological genius and spiritual wisdom.

A scholar and poet, a painter and social reformer, and, above all, a spiritual breakthrough artist, this great, brave woman has traversed so many different arenas of our life and time. One day she pursues the study of the ancient Hindu philosophies while the next she may be crawling through drug-ridden ghettos, rescuing those who are caught in the miasma of crack and heroin. Taking them back to her Ashram, she cures while she educates, ennobles while she brings them to new ways of being. Her work with those fallen to HIV/AIDS is mythic in its depth and scope. People are tended with so much love and care that, even when dying, they know their lives have been redeemed and deepened. With Ma, they have come home.

On the social frontier, Ma is also an expert of the follow-through, without which civilization would quickly lapse into entropy. She knows how things work. She has access to both the vision of the possibilities and the strategy to put them into motion. Few of her efforts are lost, many have had significant consequences in the betterment of our social reality. She assumes a kind of rightful Mother-Mind joined to an imperviousness that is not about to be caught in anything that is going to stop the drive in her. She innovates, challenges, scolds, and, above all, makes things happen.

Ultimately, Ma Jaya is about Reality in a time of so much opportunity, when the world's needs and the spiritual traditions of humanity are coming together in ways never known before. With Ma, there is in her teachings the quest for meaning, transcendence, the discipline of seeing the interrelatedness among things, compassion, goodness, laughter, and the great Pattern that connects all things with each other as well as ways to live kindly with the suffering that is an inescapable part of the human condition. With Ma, we take seriously the dictum of being renewed through the renewing of our minds, and our bodies and souls as well. The powers of Second Genesis lie within us, but this means that we must agree to attune and orchestrate our thoughts and emotions towards higher purposes and creative ends. In this we have help, for Spirit assures that the lure of becoming is always calling as is the incendiary vision of what we may be. We are limited only by concept and the refusal that comes from ignorance or laziness to remount the slope of thought.

Ma's vast experience and wisdom tells us that it is Wake-Up time and we can no longer live under the thumb of what could only be described as metaphysical sadomasochism.

With precise and clear directions she demonstrates the ways for building a new matrix of mind and manifestation. She shows us how to stop boring God by waking up to the fact that we are here in Godschool to learn the principles of world making and the evolving of self and society. Evolution is seen to follow involution wherein we discover that our minds are star gates, our bodies celled of mysteries that give us keys to the emerging phase of our existence.

There is a wonderful Sufi teaching story of a man broken-hearted by all the suffering and sorrow he saw in the world. He sat by the roadside and began to beat the earth. He looked up and yelled at God, "Look at this mess. Look at all this pain. Look at all this killing and hatred. God, Oh God, why don't you DO something!?"

And God said, "I did do something. I sent you."

The life and work of Ma Jaya is testament to this sending.

—*Dr. Jean Houston*

Scholar, philosopher and researcher in human capacities, Jean Houston is one of the foremost visionary thinkers and doers of our time, and one of the principal founders of the Human Potential Movement.

PART ONE

Karma

An Invitation

The laws of karma are the same for everyone, yet how karma works in our lives is absolutely individual. It is so specific, so intricate, so unique for each person, that for many years I did not believe I would ever be able to explain karma in a book.

Throughout the nearly forty years I've been teaching, my students and those I serve have asked me the same questions. Some questions are personal: "Why do I make the same mistakes over and over?" "Why does my life feel so small?" "Why am I depressed?" "Why do I just feel as if something's not right?" Other questions are more philosophical: "Why do innocent people suffer?" "What is true freedom?" The questions keep coming, day after day, year after year, and even more so and more urgently, today.

What all these questions have in common is karma. *Karma*—doesn't that mean some kind of inescapable eternal fate? No, but we may think this because we have misunderstood the meaning of this powerful word. This book offers a different understanding, and it offers a practical way to change your karma and therefore your life. Karma is real but you have free will. You can choose to free yourself of karma. Everyone can.

In the pages that follow, I do not advocate a religious belief, yet I explain a path to freedom and offer you a way to lessen the karmic burden you carry. The ancient roots of the idea of karma lie in India, but if this idea feels foreign to you, change the words so they fit your beliefs. It's not helpful to ask, What religion is this? Instead, ask, How can I lighten the burden of negativity that I carry? How can I release my soul to realize its true nature? What keeps me from knowing God? The path to freedom is the same even if we use different words to understand our bondage.

Now I have a question for you: What would it be like if your karma did not hold you back? Who could you be? What is stopping you from realizing your greatest potential?

What would it feel like to realize that potential? Would you like to find out?

CHAPTER ONE

What is Karma?

A Continuous Flow of Thought

We forget our freedom, but we never stop longing for it.

Do you ever wonder why you make the same mistakes over and over? Do you feel that you could be more than you are now? Do you yearn to become your true Self?

This yearning means you have forgotten something that is waiting to be awakened, and it tells you that you are more than you think you are. You long to know and become your true Self. From your misunderstanding of that yearning, you may start looking for something or someone to grab onto, something to fill the emptiness within you. When that fails, as it usually does, you look for someone to blame and, in the end, you blame yourself, which leads to self-hatred or acting out. Then it all starts again—pain, seeking, attachment, blame, self-doubt—and you are right back where you started: trapped. Over and over again, you degrade yourself by being attached to a drama that has no reality.

This is karma: the thoughts, emotions and actions that have become a pattern within your being. That pattern is your trap. Karma is a continuous flow of thought with roots in the past, and it goes on for as long as we live and beyond. It flows from moment to moment and even from lifetime to lifetime. Just as each moment contains the birth of something as well as the death of something, karma can be birthed—or broken—in any moment.

Karma is a word in general use today, yet few truly understand its real significance. A word originating in Sanskrit and used in Hinduism and Buddhism, *karma* has been translated to mean the universal law of cause and effect. Like gravity and magnetism, karma is just how the world works. Actions have consequences. Karma is reflected in common sayings: "As you sow, so shall you reap" and "What goes around comes around." Because it is a universal law, karma affects all of human life and is involved in every single thing we do or feel or think.

However, "bad" karma is not punishment or retribution, nor is "good" karma a system of rewards and prizes. Karma itself is neutral, a balancing out of the scales of universal law.

Every action may start a chain of effects that goes forward in time much farther than we can see. If you drink and drive, what is the effect of killing someone with your car? How does that person's absence change the lives of everyone around him? What results from your absence as you serve time in prison? The chain of karma reaches backward in time too. When you were a child, did you ever see your father sometimes drink and drive and get away with it? What forces shaped his life?

To try to trace the chains of karmic action and reaction is a humbling experience, for if we are honest we must soon see that we are *all* conditioned by our pasts, our childhoods, our culture, and by the very fact of being human. Notice how quickly the number of karmic possibilities accumulates beyond the amount of information the human mind can grasp. Universal mind, or God mind, has no such limits.

Birth, Death, and Breath

Karma is written on the breath.

We're all born, we all die, we all make choices, and we all carry with us the consequences of our choices. In other words, we all have karma. Karma enters into human life at birth, as the universal laws of order seep down from the great sky of consciousness to enter the human body and bind us to them. We take possession of our karma. We will either follow it blindly or learn to control our destiny by being aware of it.

Karma arrives with the very first breath, and each breath we take reflects upon the breath we have just taken. Then death comes and the breath goes out for the last time and the soul leaves the body. If you have worldly desires at the moment of death, you will write your desires on your last out breath. If you have fear, fear will go with you on the out breath. If, in one lifetime, you have left something important undone, then you will return, with last life's lessons still waiting to be learned. If you did not live your life to its fullest, you must repay that debt to yourself. Karma is how you pay.

That final exhalation of breath into death holds your karma like a clothesline, with all the clothes ready to be worn again in a familiar pattern. With the first breath into life, you inhale all that you ever were, all that you ever knew; you breathe in those same desires, those same patterns of karma, like putting on your old clothes.

Past Lives

We've all been everything.

When I was first awakening to spiritual life, I had all this energy running through me, and I needed to give it away, to serve, to work, to touch. I talked to a priest who got me a volunteer job working with children who had leukemia. In those days, these kids had very little chance of survival, at five years old, six years old. I would play with them one week, and the next week they were gone. It bothered me terribly. I had three healthy children at home, and it just seemed unfair. I was born a Jew, I was going to church with my Catholic husband, and I wasn't finding answers that satisfied my heart. When I began to hear about reincarnation, my questions began to be answered. Or, I should say, my old questions were replaced with new ones, and that's when I began to study karma.

When we begin to understand that every soul is a traveler through life and death, we start to have a deep understanding of what is real and what is not. Following Hindu and Buddhist philosophy, I have come to believe in reincarnation, even though the idea was very strange to me at first.

Is it necessary to believe in reincarnation to understand karma? No. Certainly it is not my aim to get you to accept the ideas of any particular religion. But consider this: Every night during sleep, a state that is mysterious to most of us, you die, or something within you dies. If you have made peace with your day before sleep takes you, you awaken refreshed. But if you carry a burden into sleep, the morning is laden with the same feelings you had the day before. It is similar with death and rebirth.

Some people want so much to remember their past lives that they go to psychics or they try past-life regression therapies. But if you remembered all your past lives, how would you function? Isn't it hard enough to remember where you left your car keys? Knowing everything that has happened throughout many lifetimes would overwhelm your mind. And what would you do with the information? Do you really think that if greed seeps into you, you won't act on it just because you remember how greed hurt you in a previous life? The last time you ate ice cream, you gained weight. Did you learn, and will you never eat ice cream again? Let's not kid ourselves.

Most importantly, if you did remember past deeds, do you realize the implication? If standing here in your actual present life, you knew your mistakes from the past and you went ahead and did the same things again in this life, the karmic burden would be much, much greater. Your karma, which is now loose and flowing, would turn into solid blocks of stone.

No, you can't remember your lifetimes, and you're lucky you can't. You are here. This moment means more than any other lifetime. In each lifetime, the circumstances are different. Only the patterns stay the same. Be in this one life; be in this most precious moment. Use it to conquer your confusion, your sadness, or anything that stops you from living a life of joy.

All you need to know about past lives is to recognize when something feels familiar. There is a part of you that holds a record of past lives, but it is not available to the ego mind. It is known only by your intuition and your heart, where the impressions have stayed. They will tell you when you are thinking the same old thoughts again or feeling the same old despair or doing the same old thing.

If you try to change your situation by examining it with your mind alone, you may get caught in "what if's," second thoughts, self-doubts, regrets, and blame—but did all that take you anywhere the last time you tried to think it through? Or are you right back where you started? The ego mind tends to lead us in circles.

Instead of looking at past lives, look at the life you are living now. Hear your intuition when it says, "Haven't you been here before? Aren't you tired of it?"

And ask yourself, If I died right now, would I be willing to be reborn as the exact same person as I am today? That's the question to ask, not, What did I do in my past lives? If you don't like the answer, then begin to make changes. It's a new choice every time. Every single moment is a birth; every single moment is a death. It's all in you—now! You are the ruler of your life.

Ego Arises

The ego knows only separation from God.

Karmic patterns are innate, but for karma to become active, ego must arise, and this happens soon after birth. An infant is born with a very quiet bliss that covers him or her in the womb. When the child is born, the harshness of reality breaks through and the child cries out: "I am hungry, feed me. I am uncomfortable, clothe me. I'm in need of love, love me." This feeling of need is not yet ego, attachment, or karma; it is just the simple reality of being alive.

When these needs go unmet, as surely they will at times, we allow a crack to open in the ocean of bliss; we create a separation. The very first ego thought now enters the infant mind. The ego's first thought is not "I need," but "I want," and this is the beginning of duality. Our natural state of bliss is now divided by the idea that something is missing: If I have this or that, then I'll have my bliss back. This mistaken idea takes hold. The thought "I want" now takes countless forms, countless ways to keep the soul separate from its birthright.

That's what ego is—our small self, born of forgetting, held together by hunger, and separated from bliss. This is the ego as it is understood in most Eastern philosophies, although Western psychology uses the word differently.

In its failure to remember anything greater than itself, the ego acts out of its own willfulness. It is through the ego's willful actions that karma is birthed. Day to day, lifetime to lifetime, karma accumulates. With this accumulation, patterns emerge as the ego makes the same mistakes over and over. Then karma solidifies.

Ego is the aspect of the individual self that keeps us limited, confused, and out of touch with the universal Self. Ego and karma are closely linked: The greater the karma, the bigger the ego. The bigger the ego, the more karma clings to it. That's why the goal of many spiritual practices is to loosen our habit of identifying ourselves with the ego.

Craving

The hungry heart has no beginning and no end.

Desire for the great sea of bliss that we felt as newborns begins to spread out in the form of attachments. The primal hunger for this oneness gets tangled up with our hunger for lesser things. Attachment is often confused with love, but this kind of love is only possession.

What if we were attached to everything in our lives and clutched so tight we didn't let our lives breathe? What if we clutched at our children, our possessions, our ideas, our religion, to life itself? Could we even recognize our original bliss?

The child who once knew bliss can spend his whole life searching for wholeness and clutching at illusions. He may have hunger growing so deep in his heart that, as he grows older, he will look everywhere *but* in that heart to fulfill the yearning that he feels.

Perhaps you were raised in poverty, or perhaps your youth was comfortable but devoid of love. Thus, you don't know how to create love or accept love, so you search all your life and you cannot find it. What *do* you find? Food. Drugs. Alcohol. Dependency on someone who hurts you. So many things to find in the world! You may even find religion to fill up the hungry heart. But something is still missing.

The hunger, still burning within you, moves from one moment to the next, from night into day, from one life to the next. It is powerful and demands to be taken care of; the thirst must be quenched. In the quest for what you think you need, you sometimes hurt others, even if you try not to. And so, new karma forms. Hunger drives you, then regret drives you. Yet the hunger continues, this craving for oneness that takes on many disguises. In the end the question for some of us comes down to this: Where is God? We do remember God—but we remember in the form of a great hunger.

Then you may ask, How did God let this happen? How did God let me become an alcoholic, or obese, or so terribly depressed? How did God let me waste my life in the pursuit of pleasures that don't last? Eventually you may give up on God, or the hunger itself may become your god.

We are all given glimpses of a higher reality, whether we choose to act on them or not. There are times when we are reminded of the primal bliss, times when we sometimes dare to believe that freedom and wholeness are possible. By then, most of us have gotten used to our karmically conditioned life and we've become comfortable. We settle into this place of comfort because it is familiar. Even pain can be comfortable, compared with the fear of the unknown. When we move too far toward freedom, we become afraid.

Perhaps you've moved a little closer to your heart's goal—to Christ, to universal spirit, to the gods and goddesses of any tradition—or maybe you've just grown closer to love, to kindness, to beauty, to whatever it is that will awaken you to the very truth of who you are. *And then you back away.*

We are torn between fear and longing. Meanwhile, the karmic ties keep tightening.

Karmic Patterns

The ego plants seeds of suffering
and waters them with self-doubt.

Even a tiny baby determines how tightly her own past karma will wrap around her. How completely will she identify with duality as it arises? How quickly will she forget the oneness? How eager will she be to embrace the attachments of earth? It's certainly not a rational choice—it's not even a choice of the conscious mind—but there is choice nevertheless.

After we have tasted duality and the beginnings of ego, and after our old karma has settled in to surround our souls, new karma now has a place to cling. We create new karma through our own actions. But as young children, before our actions carry full karmic consequences, we encounter the judgments of others: "You're clumsy." "You're just like your father." Or perhaps judgment hasn't even been spoken, but we feel it.

Karma adheres to karma. Picture how Velcro sticks to itself but not to a smooth surface. Karma works like that.

If, for example, you have a karmic pattern that consists of you continually telling yourself that you're no good, then you will embrace every experience that reinforces this belief and reject every experience that challenges it. As children we constantly pick up clues about who we are. We absorb these clues, developing deep habits that hold karmic value; in other words, they have grown a karmic root. For example, a child proudly brings a drawing home from school and her mother ignores it, once, twice, ten times. Every child eventually gets a message from this. A child who has a deep pre-existing karmic root of self-doubt will be more deeply wounded than one who doesn't. She will think that she isn't worthy of her mother's time. She may stop drawing and never return to it again. But another child, without such a root, may not feel it so deeply.

We absorb others' beliefs about us until we are conditioned to believe in our false personalities, which we continue to build ever more elaborately as our lives unfold. After a while we just ride the waves made by the judgments of others, allowing them to take us where they will.

Meanwhile, beliefs give rise to actions, which in turn become habits. Thus, we create new karma. Karma arises in our interactions with people. The rule is simple: If you hurt someone, you will have to pay for it. If you cause pain, you will have pain. As the ego carries out its projects, its plans for getting what it wants in the world, new karma is laid down over the old and becomes intricately entwined with it. We become ever more tangled up in karma.

The *Rig Veda*, an ancient sacred text from India, calls these patterns *samskaras*. They are not ordinary habits, but habits you do over and over and over again until they feel like part of your psyche, part of your being, something you have had with you always, because indeed you have. At the base of them, further back than the pains of childhood, and beyond the reach of psychotherapy, there is a karmic root. So to give up a root feels like you're giving up a part of yourself.

No matter what words we use to describe the process, our ego minds use our karmic patterns to trap us in a small life. We are well and truly stuck! We are conditioned by our childhood and our culture, we find ourselves in a world where most events are beyond our control, and when we seek freedom, fear grabs us. Is freedom even possible?

As long as we bounce along in the world of action and reaction, the answer is no, we are not free. We will need to look at a hidden dimension of our lives, where karma has no power. That dimension is the soul.

Destiny and the Soul

Your soul is waiting to be remembered.

The scriptures of every religion tell us we have free choice, but if everything is conditioned by previous actions, who or what can stand apart from destiny long enough to choose, or to lay claim to, our freedom? The answer is the soul. In its perfection, the soul has no characteristics, it conceives of no time, and it perceives no duality between heaven and earth, the physical and the spiritual, itself and its maker. It is simply what it is and was always: perfection. Hindus call it the *Jiva-atman*, the individual soul, because they know it to be part of the great *Atman*, the universal soul. As we enter into the world of life, of earth, of breath, we begin in the womb to put the physical around the soul—bone, blood, arteries, veins, skin, and *mind*. Duality arises, and we forget the perfection and simplicity of the soul.

While the soul, in its perfection, can't be touched by darkness, its radiance can become darkened by clouds of karma. Our deeds add to, or subtract from, these clouds. However, this is not the same as sin, and karma is not punishment; it is just the way the universe works.

Everything is destined, or everything is conditioned—everything except the soul. It is the soul that overcomes destiny, and it is the soul that chooses freedom. With the soul's perfect knowing, it can recognize itself; it can also recognize ego's choices as what they are: separation from the universal soul.

Paying Again

If you learn from one mistake,
then you can learn from all mistakes.

God loves you, and the universe embraces you, just as you are right now, in your soul's perfection. If you live well, if you try not to hurt anyone, you will burn off past karma in a natural process; it's all very fluid. But you can make it solid by denying or forgetting the karmic lessons you already learned and repeating the same actions again and again. It's as though you bought your groceries, paid for them, loaded everything into the car, and then went back in and said, "Here's another hundred dollars." You just hand that money to the clerk, but you get nothing for it; your packages are already in the car.

You already paid for this life. You already breathed—*lived*—life's great mistakes of anger or jealousy or pride or desire, and here you are. Why keep paying?

If you relive parts of your life by blindly repeating old patterns without awareness, you will suffer the same consequences and you will pay over and over for the same mistakes. You will become imbalanced. Paying again for that which you have already paid compounds the karma or the negative tension. The karma that is fluid then becomes solidified, and from that solid material you build stepping stones for yourself that make it easy to follow what's familiar, easy to walk along the path of your predetermined destiny, easy to forget free will.

No Excuses, No Blame

God does not judge. Do you?

Sometimes we try to hide behind karma because it's comforting to think, It must be my karma to have cancer, so there's nothing I can do about it. This is illusion. You are responsible for your life now, karma or no karma. Everyone will experience pain at some point. How you deal with it is your responsibility. Hiding behind karma takes you out of your own life.

I have seen people make themselves miserable because they blame themselves. "I'm sick because I am so negative," they say. Then they train themselves in positive affirmations in the hope of curing themselves. If that fails, they only blame themselves more and spiral down into despair. They miss the point by confusing responsibility with blame. Cancer happens, accidents happen, misfortune strikes; sometimes we can recognize the causes, but often the reasons are unfathomable. Whatever the cause, karmic or not, blaming yourself will not create the freedom you seek.

Gradually, through awareness, it is possible to develop a feel for your own karma and how it acts in your life. Once you can recognize it, you can start to unravel it. However, you can never know or understand anyone else's karma.

Many people make the mistake of judging others who are suffering. They tell themselves, "Those children must have bad karma, or else they wouldn't be orphans." Believing that you understand the karma of others makes it easy to judge them. To think you know the mind of God or the mind of the universe becomes an excuse to not help the suffering.

Karma can cause suffering, yet not in the way you might think. I'm always asked questions such as, "If a baby dies in a plane crash, is that his karma?" Sometimes it is, but rarely. You would have to believe that all three hundred people on the plane had the same karma, and somehow they all decided to get on the same airplane together. That's just not how it works.

Yes, there is cause and effect, and perhaps, in the big picture, lifetime after lifetime, time beyond comprehension, there has been a specific karmic root of every bad and good thing that happens, but so what? Does it really help you to know? Even if your mind could trace that baby's karma all the way back to the very beginning, how does it help either you or the baby? It doesn't; it just distracts you from what you need to do.

Good Karma, Bad Karma, No Karma

Good karma may make us happy,
but it does not make us free.

Karma accumulates, both the positive and the negative. Our natural state is to be one with God, or in tune with the ultimate spirit, and all karma suppresses this oneness as it creates separation. Anything you bring in from past lifetimes or even the past years of this lifetime weighs heavy on the soul, whether good or bad. The goal is to become empty of karma, positive as well as negative.

Karma explains why one person is born with a gift for music and another with a gift for carpentry. It explains how young children can manifest extraordinary abilities. We say that they have a gift, forgetting that the gift came from themselves. Although good karma may seem to be a great gift, it can actually unbalance your life and hold you back. We would be better off with no karma at all, just living the purity of the soul. Until we reach that state, it's important to use good karma wisely.

If you take your talents for granted or rely on them and just coast through life, you fail to take on life's challenges and learn new things. Your life may become flat or one-sided. You may feel as if you are in a rut. This is a karmic pattern as well.

If you have a gift that you do not use, if you are not where you are supposed to be in life, if you have neglected to nourish your talents, you experience great pain. This seems paradoxical—the goal is to free ourselves of both good and bad karma, yet we must also be sure to develop our karmic gifts. How can we do both?

Find karmic balance by doing what is new to you, even if it might be challenging. Try not to travel the same old road; welcome the movement of change. Develop new gifts, or add to the old, and, above all, be sure to share your talents. Take care that you don't become stuck running along the same old track, positive or negative. You can free yourself from good karma, not through self-denial but through gratitude for the gifts given you, by sharing your good fortune, and by finding ways to grow in new directions. In this way, you will move towards freedom from karma of all kinds and toward the emptiness and contentment that is your birthright.

Karmic Boredom

You are not your past.

We are comfortable repeating familiar patterns, and after many years we become so exhausted that we're not even walking the path anymore. Instead, the path is walking us. Nothing changes. A new day, a new year, a new lifetime, and yet accumulated karma has seeped into the present moment, and at some point we know that what we're doing is going to have the same result that it had before. Maybe *you* don't know this, in your conscious mind. Yet at the cellular level, your thoughts, your actions, your reactions may become just as steady and predictable as the action of your heart and lungs. When you cling to that which you already know and hide from the new, the cells of your life become overloaded, and with that comes pain, disease and addiction in all its forms. There's a flatness to everything you do. That's karmic boredom.

When you awaken each morning with this karmic boredom, you may sigh, "Just another day." You feel you've seen it all, and in a sense you have. Yet, if you learn to live in the present moment, every morning is brand new. Maybe there's an interesting cloud in the sky, maybe there's a quarter moon, maybe there are raindrops, maybe there's a sparrow chirping, or a squirrel running. Every single moment is a birth. Every single moment is a death.

So what happens when you have the choice to do something new in your life? This is when you can choose freedom. This is when you can let your intuition speak to you, if you've learned to quiet your mind: I've been here before. I won't do the same thing again.

Another Way: The Gap

When you are in the moment, you are in eternity.

There is a gap in the universal order, there is a gap in karma, and that gap allows you to change your destiny. It is the *Now*.

Our existence is a continuation, a weaving through three states. There is life, there is death, and there is the little space between life and death, or between death and life. In that space are all possibilities, not yet crystallized into destiny, a gap in the universal order. This fluid state occurs not just in the space between life and death. There are many of these gaps, interpenetrating all time and all matter. This is why there is free will, and this is why the world does not run only in the tracks of destiny.

Everything moves, everything changes, all things flow. Compared to the past and future, the present moment seems fleeting, insubstantial, ungraspable, so we let it go by. But reality has a dimension of depth in both space and time, and time is not as we perceive it. In the transitions between life and death, in meditation, in prayer, in mystical experience, even in the space between breaths, the present moment blooms forth and we can become aware. Awareness is not past, it is not future, it is not some after-death state. Awareness is now. It is the key to freedom.

The gap, the moment, is outside of time.

When the ego comes and pulls you away from the moment, you are returned to the conditioned world of cause and effect, which is the world of karma. You are bound again by both ego and time. It is the limited concept of time that makes us confuse karma with destiny.

However, our innate wisdom presents itself in the moment of hesitation. I don't mean indecision or procrastination; I mean the tiny hesitation before action that offers the choice of not blindly following your destiny. This is the moment where intuition says yes or no, before every action, large or small. This power of hesitation represents the higher mind in battle with the lower mind. The higher mind longs for freedom; the lower mind, controlled by ego, clings to its habits. If you hesitate and use that moment to refuse the ego its will, you can change your destiny.

When you place yourself with awareness between that which is and that which was, even in seemingly small choices, you force the universal godhead to open a path so alien to your old destiny that *you* can then take control. You have found a gap in the universal order. You have willed yourself to find grace. The perfection of that universal order that was birthed in the heavens now rains upon you through free will. Your whole being shudders with anticipation and the thought of taking another way.

Find Your Soul

The soul speaks to us again and again, if we listen.

The ego keeps us trapped in our karmas. But you can learn to listen to your soul instead of your ego. The first step is to develop your awareness so that you recognize the karmic gaps when they arise. Your mind, a creature of karma, chatters along missing chance after chance. Start by quieting the chatter of the mind through meditation.

The goal of meditation is to open a space within your being that is outside your mind. Through meditation, awareness will grow, the gaps will become clear, and you will begin to unravel your karma. You will become the master of your destiny. There are many ways to meditate, and I will say more about them as we go on. As you grow in awareness, you will hear the voice of the soul speaking to you of compassion, of courage, and of kindness to yourself and others. Listen to it.

The Physical Connection

Karma can block the free flow of energy.

Karma has a physical connection to our bodies as well as our minds. There are seven main energy centers, or chakras, in the body. Spiritual energy flows upward from the base of the spine to the top of the head, and each chakra expresses a different part of our being.

The first chakra, at the base of the spine, connects us to the beauty of the earth. The second chakra, located in the area of the sexual and reproductive organs, governs creativity. The third chakra, located at the solar plexus, is the seat of our personal power. Some systems of yoga refer to these three as the "lower" chakras, and some teachings advise us to avoid them. However, all chakras contain light, all are connected, and eventually all will come into balance.

The fourth chakra, in the center of the chest, is the home of love and compassion. The fifth chakra, in the throat, is where we use words, art, or music to express everything we have learned on our journey. The sixth chakra is located in the center of the forehead. It is comprised of thousands of particles of light, and it enables us to perceive Spirit more directly. The seventh chakra, at the crown of the head, is where freedom from the small self begins as we become one with the ultimate reality.

Quite simply, karma affects the way our chakras work. Visualize the chakras as turning wheels of light one above another, from the base of the spine to the top of the head. Now imagine that someone comes along and jams a stick in between the spokes of one of the wheels. That's what karma does: stops you short and keeps you stuck.

There are three places where we most easily notice the blockages made by karma, because we can feel them as physical tension in the solar plexus, the chest, and the throat, each corresponding to one of the chakras. Make a habit of checking with your body to sense any blocked energy. This can lead you to an awareness of where you have become stuck.

Pieces of a Puzzle

The moment of truth comes when
what you want is what you need.

Imagine that all your lifetimes together make up one great puzzle. In each individual lifetime, you have the task of completing one section of the puzzle. Sometimes when something just feels off in your life, even if nothing specifically is wrong, it's because you are karmically imbalanced—you can feel it intuitively. You feel as if there is more you must be or do because you aren't working on the puzzle.

To find the pieces of your life's puzzle, the real questions you must ask are these:

- Am I focused on what I want instead of what I need?
- What shall I do with this life that has been given to me?
- How will I develop my intuition to recognize the right choices when they come to me?
- How can I refrain from causing harm?
- How will I sustain the ability to be kind to others?

22

- Who can I serve?

- How can I develop the quiet within myself so that I can find the answers to my questions?

Seek your inner answers, and you will begin to have a new understanding of what you truly need in your life. Gradually what you want will begin to match up with what you need. Instead of living a dead life of mental chatter and obsessions, or a sterile life that is just a cycle of desires and addictions, you will have a new life, a very alive life.

As you begin to recognize karma around you, it can feel as if you stepped into a different universe. The old rules don't apply, you see your problems with new eyes, and nothing is quite what you thought it was. It's almost like seeing double—the eyes of the ego see the world one way, the eyes of the soul see something quite different.

All that exists is inside you. All that you seek is available. There is a life, a death, and a resurrection in every moment, in every molecule, in every breath.

CHAPTER TWO

What is a Karmic Space?

Karmic Spaces: Walls in Your Mind

You have created your own walls.

The creations of the ego mind lead us into places that we cannot easily escape. In its repetition of patterns, its obsessions, its clinging, and its cravings, the mind arranges for its own entrapment. The walls of the mind were created by karma. Now karma says to us, "You are what you were; you will be what you are now." Fortunately, the soul responds, "But you don't have to be."

It's true, you always have choice. Since we have built these walls, we have the power to take them apart. However, thought and reason quickly reach their limits when faced with karma and its web of connections. This is why I have distilled all the thousands of ways the ego entraps us down to eleven specific types of karmic patterns. I call them "karmic spaces" because they are where the mind habitually flees. They represent the cycles of the repetition and reinforcement of karma.

The karmic spaces seem to be places of shelter, seductive in their familiarity, because we are more comfortable where we have walked for many lifetimes, seeking the same path in our hearts, our minds, and our bones. Sometimes I call them the "karmic cubbyholes." Just the way Velcro is a good representation of how karma sticks to itself, the concept of cubbyholes describes how the karmic spaces all line up, like the mail slots behind the front desk in an old-fashioned hotel. Think of a row of little dark boxes—narrow, yet somehow warm and inviting, like cozy nests.

These are the places you climb into because they are so familiar, and their familiarity rests on karmic patterns.

We can find ourselves caught in any one of the eleven different karmic spaces at any given moment, or in several at the same time. Every karmic space seems hopeless when we are mired in it, and just when we think we have found the exit, we discover that we are still entangled in the same old circular pattern of action and reaction. This is what distinguishes a deep karmic pattern from a passing cloud of emotion.

Continuing to be stuck in our lives, repeating the same patterns, yet expecting different results, is exactly what keeps us from finding our true nature. Freeing ourselves from the karmic spaces brings us out of duality and into oneness (or if you prefer, into alignment with God's will or with our connection to source). I use the word *God* interchangeably with terms from many traditions. Theologians may find fault with this, but all these words are just shorthand for the ultimate reality, or the ultimate spirit. That's why I always tell my students: "If any of these words or phrases feel foreign to you, substitute your own words, your own beliefs." The reality remains the same.

The karmic spaces can never confine the soul—nothing can—but they can confine the small self that yearns to become one with the universal soul. We could count thousands of these traps of the mind, but here they are distilled to eleven. The purpose of naming them is so that you can become more aware when they are at work in your life. Recognize them, take responsibility for them, understand them, and you will take back your free will, your karma, and your life. The eleven karmic spaces are:

- Jealousy
- Anger
- Pride
- Indifference
- Ego of self-thought and self-indulgence

26

- Lack of awareness
- Intent
- Worldly desires
- Abuse of power
- Desire to be right
- Attachment

In Part Two, we will look deeply at each of the eleven karmic spaces and how we can break free of the patterns that hold us back and cause suffering. But first, let's look at how to get the most out of this book.

How to Use This Book

Freeing yourself from karma is an individual journey. This book will work best as a guide for you to simply examine your life today. Go easy on yourself. You don't have to be on some strict spiritual path to understand yourself and your patterns a bit better. Where you are in your life now, that's where you begin.

Learning about the karmic spaces will help you recognize yourself, both your ego and your higher Self. Each chapter on the eleven karmic spaces includes:

- "Recognizing the Karmic Space," which helps you identify the particular karmas you struggle with and shows you many ways to easily recognize when you're in a karmic space.
- "Karmic Connections." All karmas are connected. Understanding these connections can help free you.
- "Karmic Graces." These are the positive aspects that help you to get out of a space by replacing negativity. They are graces because as you develop them they will stay with you and enhance your life.

- "Practices for Letting Go." These are short exercises to help you release the ego's grip on the mind. They will soothe the chaos of your thoughts so it's easier to slip out of a space once you know you're stuck.
- Stories by students about their experiences with the karmic spaces are interspersed throughout the chapters.

Let's look at how each of these sections contributes to a deeper understanding of a karmic space and how to transform it.

Recognizing The Karmic Spaces

We are used to figuring out our lives with our minds, and we keep trying and trying, even after we discover the mind's tendency to take us around in a circle. For example, you may have left a bad relationship, but a year later you begin to see that your new relationship is a lot like the old one. You try to analyze what went wrong, but instead you are flooded with negative thoughts: "What's wrong with me?" "I'll never find love," and so on. You saw a pattern, but you didn't recognize its karmic roots, and so you were powerless to change it deeply enough to make a difference.

The eleven karmic spaces offer a new way to see the deeper patterns and change them. Recognizing the karmic spaces begins with intuition, which is really your soul's deep wisdom. As you look back over your life with the eyes of the soul, you'll begin to see your karma. The section called "Recognizing the Karmic Space" at the beginning of each chapter will help you open your eyes to your patterns so you can identify them—the first step to freedom.

Karmic Connections

The karmic spaces are connected to each other. There is a flow and interweaving of karmic thoughts and actions among them, which is why karma sometimes feels like a hopeless tangle. It doesn't really matter how you visualize your way out of karma, whether you see it as unraveling a tangle or as escaping from a box. The reality is the same: All karma is connected.

From the first karmic space of jealousy, for example, you can slip easily into resentment and then into the second karmic space, anger. Now you've brought pain to your own heart, causing a protective crust to grow around it so that you cannot feel when you hurt others. This can result in indifference or the isolation of pride. The desire to be right can lead to anger, and vice versa. Within the space of anger, you may connect to the desire for revenge. Complaining is a connecting karma within the ego of self-thought and self-indulgence. It goes on and on and round and round.

As you can see, it is easy to slip out of one space into another, or to find yourself in more than one space at a time. But, similarly, once you realize that you are stuck in one space, it becomes easier to stop yourself from going into another space. These sections will describe additional patterns within each karmic space.

FEAR AND NEGATIVITY

Learn to develop a positive thought in a dark moment.

There are two karmas that pay rent in every space and do the most damage: fear and negativity. Fear keeps you on the path of the old. It stifles your new-found awareness and your deepest yearnings. Due to fear, you may become that most pain-filled of beings, an "almost"—almost happy, almost free, almost liberated, and always torn between fear and longing.

Fear is our necessary response to danger, so it comes and goes in our lives as a natural warning system. Fear in itself is not karma, but it contributes to karma when it feeds on itself, spiraling out of control, freezing us up, stopping us from moving. When fear holds us in its grip like that, it is old fear that, through long repetition, has become karmic fear.

Another powerful karma is the habit of negative thinking. We tend to listen to the ego, which says to every cell in our being, "Stillness is boring; movement and thinking negative thoughts are exciting." Meanwhile, negative thoughts make us hunched over and contracted so we fit ever more easily into the karmic spaces. Negativity is how the ego puts a stop to our natural state of being aware of goodness and wholeness, as well as the joy of life.

There are many negative thought patterns, including judgment, self-judgment, depression, guilt … the list goes on. We will look at each of these in the chapters that follow, but the first thing to realize is that they are just thoughts and emotions, which come and go, arise and pass away, all part of the flow of life. Thoughts have no roots, unless we plant and nurture them.

We hear a lot about the power of positive thinking, and it's mostly true. The hard part, though, is to train ourselves to make a conscious choice and to choose freedom when everything in us is screaming in pain. One of the greatest lessons I ever learned was how to develop a positive thought in a dark moment.

Karmic Graces

Every karmic space holds within it positive aspects and lessons of great value for your life. I call them "karmic graces." The graces not only lead you out of a space, but they are the gift of the space. This is because usually you have to use just a tiny bit of a grace in order to get out of the space you are stuck in. As you do, you help that grace unfold in your life.

Visualize the karmic cubbyholes, these narrow mail slots where we like to hide out in the dark. On the walls of these spaces are written all your chaotic thoughts, thoughts that have no meaning whatsoever because they are based in fear and negative thinking. When most of us are afraid or in pain, it feels natural to go deeper into the tight space that is most familiar to us, until we go so deep that we can't find a way out. Despair, depression, hopelessness—these are some of the words we use to describe how we feel when we are stuck.

This is because the karmic cubbyholes have no back doors. That means, to escape, you have to go out the same way you went in, by facing your deepest fears. But usually what happens is that you just get yourself in deeper, moving all the way to the back wall, looking for a way out. What do you find? Not an exit, but still there is hope, because bunched up against that back wall are all the positive aspects of the cubbyhole.

To put it another way, with karma you must grasp the reality of your predicament before you reach for grace. Most important, know that in every karmic space there is light, a little speck of light, like a candle. The graces are what lead us out of a space. They are the lights that show us the way—but you must reach for them. Pick up the light of grace, fan the flame of awareness, turn around and look at your demons, look at what hurts you, confuses you, entraps you, and go back the way you came.

There are many graces, but five in particular can serve as keys to every karmic space: Awareness, Intuition, Faith, Discipline, and Compassion.

AWARENESS

The ego cannot hide in the light of awareness,
and neither can karma.

The mind can easily be taken over by the ego unless you are in control of your life and your breath. Therefore, learn to see things that you have taken for granted. Be mindful of your physical world and your spiritual world. Be mindful of your body and your ability to smile. Truly look at the colors of life around you and see how bright they become right before your eyes. Spiritual seekers of every tradition and path have been told, "Know thyself," "The unexamined life is not worth living," or, in the *Tao Te Ching*, "It is wisdom to know others; it is enlightenment to know one's self." Yet, the ego stops us from discovering the inner life and blocks us from knowing the ultimate truth of who we are. For retreat and contemplation, the Buddha sat under the Bodhi tree, Jesus went into the desert, countless men and women through the ages have chosen to live out their lives in seclusion in caves or monasteries.

Are you not quite ready for the monastery? That's OK, because karma is the law of action. The best place to understand your karma is by becoming aware of it in your life now. I have never advised my students to go off and be in solitude. We live on this earth in this time, so I tell them, "Be in the world, but put your hands together in prayer, and then use those same hands to serve someone."

Cultivating awareness requires practice, but as your awareness expands, one day you might be surprised to see how much becomes clear to you that you never understood before. You will begin to notice in the reflection of your own being that something has entered into your life, something big and wonderful. You will be surprised to find yourself surpassing your own potential and overcoming the obstacles that you have created for yourself. You will begin to understand the nature of all things, and your heart will be stretched to let in more compassion for yourself and others. You will become the expert on your own feelings and your own karmic patterns.

INTUITION

Intuition is a spiritual art.

The vibration of yesterday's karma comes into today like a spear thrown by the ego. This old energy distorts the vibration of the present and causes you to do the same thing over and over. But it is your intuition that allows you to sense the patterns of karma as they form and repeat themselves, so it is intuition that can unravel your karma and set you free. Sadly, the more you distrust your intuition, the more you mistrust your soul, the more you make mistakes with your life and the lives of others.

The soul gives birth to intuition. Because the soul is perfect, your intuition is always right. But watch how it works: This just feels *so right*, you tell yourself, and off you go to do something foolish. If you're like some of my students, pretty soon you come back looking much the worse for wear, and you say to me, "But you said intuition is always right." Yes, it is; but only if you have taken the time to learn, to understand, and to trust intuition correctly; only if you remember that the ego knows how to hijack every positive ability.

There is a universal mind that has all the answers. It comes to you as a vibration. You can't connect to universal mind with thought, only with the vibration of love. To develop intuition requires that you learn how to listen to your heart's mind through the stillness of meditation. Then, with your own knowledge and wisdom, the truth of who you are and your soul's knowing will burst forth.

FAITH

Where there is faith, there is only
the destiny that you chose to have.

Like awareness, faith is a light that always burns, with or without your acknowledgment. Always there, it urges you on in the darkness. In the darkest space that you go into, the light of faith is there to remind you that you never have to stay where you are. Faith in what? you ask. Is this turning into a religion? No, but have faith in yourself.

If you meditate, if you pray, or even if you simply acknowledge the higher power that is in you, then you will be a carrier of the simplest form of faith. That faith is your natural ability to come out of the darkest corner, the darkest space, and the darkest time of the heart. When you find yourself caught in such a space, say a prayer. Never mind if you intellectually believe in prayer or not, never mind if you think of a higher reality as inside you or outside—just do it. You will find that faith holds more power than the seductions of any karmic space.

DISCIPLINE

Stop!

To live fully is to be in each moment. This requires that you conquer the ego thoughts and desires that encourage you to flee into the karmic spaces when life is difficult. Conquer your anger, conquer your desires, conquer your confusion and attachment by embracing self-discipline. You can do this now, without knowing anything else for sure, only having a feeling that this way leads toward your highest Self.

Discipline? The very word provokes resistance. You may think of discipline as lack of freedom, but this too is the ego's illusion. In truth, discipline leads to freedom, bringing you security in yourself and keeping you out of the trap of procrastination. Through discipline you learn control. Loss of control is the ego's leash on you.

The most important discipline is non-reaction, a tiny pause or hesitation–the gap–before action. It offers the choice of not blindly following your karma. This is the moment when your intuition says yes or no, before any action, large or small. Hesitation is powerful because in this moment, the higher mind does battle with the lower mind. The higher mind longs for freedom; the lower mind clings to its habits. If you hesitate and use that moment to refuse the lower mind its will, you enter the karmic gap, the moment of choice that allows you to step aside from your conditioned habits, the moment where you can actually change your destiny. Our soul's wisdom presents itself in the moment of hesitation. When you take the simple step to breathe and to pause, you are able to hear that wisdom.

If we act just to make ourselves comfortable in the short term, it's easy to make a mistake. I often tell the story of a monastery where the gardener was always making trouble, always starting fights with the monks. One day, his boss just fired him and all the monks breathed a sigh of relief. The next day, the head monk looked out the window and asked, "Where is the gardener?"

"He's gone. We fired him."

"You fools, you fired your liberation!"

What did he mean? In their daily dealings with the gardener, the monks had many opportunities to practice non-reaction, which could have freed them.

COMPASSION

Compassion is the religion of the heart.

We are all strangers at birth, yet we are bound together. We have all been everything and everyone. Today, you are not that homeless person passing on the street, but you might have been hungry and alone once and you could very well be again— whether in this lifetime or in other lifetimes. When we understand this, we learn to be guided by compassion.

Choosing compassion over judgment loosens karma because it guides us to stop worrying about ourselves and to take care of someone else. When we truly step into someone else's shoes, even for a moment, our personal karma doesn't go with us. This is why compassion, like hesitation, can open a gap in the karmic order.

You can practice compassion as a spiritual exercise. Make the effort to do one kind action every day, something you wouldn't normally do, like saying hello to someone you usually ignore. Just the effort will make you more aware, and as you become more aware, you will naturally become more compassionate.

Practices for Letting Go

Spiritual practices of many paths, both ancient and modern, have one common goal: to tame the mind and the chaos of thought. These practices may also open the heart or develop intuition, but none of this is possible until the mind relaxes.

Awareness always frees the mind and allows us to escape the karmic cubbyholes. But sometimes, we can be aware and still be stuck. Then it is useful to have a regular practice. When we do a practice, the mind becomes preoccupied so that the ego loses its grip on it, even just a little bit.

In each chapter on the karmic spaces are several practices to help free you from that space. There is an old tradition of doing a practice for forty days at a time. If you can make that commitment, and keep it, you will end up restoring your faith in yourself. If you can't, it doesn't matter. Every effort you make will pick up one thread of karma and show you how to unravel it. The basic practices involve the following:

- Meditation
- Breath awareness
- Prayer
- Mantra and affirmation
- Visualization
- Journaling
- Action: service, ritual, conscious movement, and yoga

MEDITATION

Karma exists in time. Meditation allows time to stop.

Your whole being is starved for the wisdom you already possess. The essential Self is calm, pure and relaxed. But in most of us, this is buried! Meditation helps you find it.

Meditation is pre-action instead of re-action. It is how you train yourself to live in the moment. Instead of always contemplating your past or your future, instead of letting the mind play with time, meditation lets it stop slowly. In that temporary suspension of mind, you also suspend karma and find another gap in the karmic order.

You won't quite grasp this until you try it, so set yourself the intention of developing a daily practice of meditation, even if it's just five minutes a day. Meditation is not about having spiritual experiences. In fact, most of the time it's boring, but that's fine.

BREATH AWARENESS

As you practice awareness of your breath,
you are practicing awareness of all of life.

Many of us just assume that breathing is an automatic process, nothing we need to pay attention to. Remember, though, that the word *spirit* is derived from the Latin word for breath. No matter how lost you may feel, your breath is always with you, and the essence of who you are is written on the breath. Once you learn to deliberately steady your breath, your life changes. Once you can breathe with awareness, what you don't need in your life just disperses.

You may have already realized the importance of being aware of your breath while doing yoga, tai chi, or any other type of conscious movement, or you may have learned breath control while practicing relaxation, massage, or pain-reduction techniques. Breath awareness is also an important element in meditation, helping us center ourselves and quiet our minds.

We can also intentionally control the breath using practices derived from the ancient science of *pranayama*, which teaches us how specific breathing patterns can be used to affect the body, mind, emotions, and states of awareness.

There are a number of breathing exercises in the "Practices for Letting Go" sections of the chapters that follow. Be gentle as you perform these practices. Check with your doctor if you are pregnant or have a health condition. If you feel yourself straining, then modify the practice or choose a different way to increase your awareness.

PRAYER

Prayer is speaking to God. Meditation is listening to God.

When you go into a church, a temple, a mosque, or when you visit any holy place, you can feel it—the accumulation of hope, prayers, worship, and the deep awareness of life and death. So many have gone before you with such deep longing and faith that, after so many years, the very air of these places brings a newness and depth to the heart. The constant prayer generates its own vibration. Eventually it all adds up.

In the same way that prayer can accumulate in a holy place, it can accumulate in your heart. From year to year or lifetime to lifetime, it gathers force and power. The spirit is immortal and so is every prayer ever uttered.

When you pray, you must understand that someone is listening. You are heard and prayers are answered, though not always in the way you expect. Take care not to let your prayers become automatic. The greatest prayer is the simplicity of your own voice talking to God in any form or non-form that feels true for you. If you pray with a sincere heart, your life will change.

MANTRA AND AFFIRMATION

Mantra opens up space inside of you.

Awareness of the power of sound is something we have lost a little bit in the West, but it is known in many ancient paths. It is based on the understanding that the universe is made up of vibration and so are we. By repeating certain words in a special phrase known as a *mantra*, you are tuning your awareness to a higher plane, much as you tune in to a radio station. In India, mantras are usually the name of a deity. You don't have to believe in the deities, as the power of the mantra is there anyway.

Prayers should not become automatic, but repetition of a mantra does become automatic after a time. As it is said, "At first you say the mantra, then let the mantra say you." Bring it into consciousness from time to time, in particular when you need to break the hold of obsessive thoughts. Let the mantra become louder than any negative thoughts. Let it drown them out and wash them away.

Affirmations are positive statements that you make to yourself and to the universe—"God loves me," for example. You say it repetitively, much like a mantra, so that it begins to wear new grooves in the tracks of your mind, running in the background, so that it can come to conscious awareness when you need it.

VISUALIZATION

If you can change your pattern just once,
you can loosen karma's repetitive grip on you.

Meditation practitioners all over the world know the power of visualization. So do athletes, who visualize every inch of the course before they run. In teaching yoga, I tell my students to modify the postures as they need to, but watch the teacher and visualize themselves doing the full asana. Even someone lying in a hospital bed can do mental yoga and get physical benefits. Scientists have identified mirror neurons in the brain, which translate what we see, including what we visualize, into physical changes.

Some people use visualization more easily than others, but it is a skill that can be developed. Over time you will begin to see new ways, and sometimes you will choose a new path.

JOURNALING

In every karmic space there is a whisper of enlightenment.

We don't always know what we're thinking until we express it. Keeping a journal helps us see our thought patterns, either in the moment through a practice like brainstorming, or over a period of time. As you become more aware of your passing thoughts, you will be surprised at the things you tell yourself all day long.

ACTION: SERVICE, RITUAL, CONSCIOUS MOVEMENT, AND YOGA

"Just do it."

The word *karma* means action, and karma yoga is the path of action. I loved it when Nike came out with "Just do it" as a slogan, because it is perfect for spiritual life as well as sports. Just meditate, just do your mantra, just be kind, and just get up off your couch (or even your meditation cushion) and help someone.

There are recommended practices in this book that ask you to take action. They may include ritual or devotional practices, where action comes together with prayer and visualization. Or they could involve conscious movement or yoga. These will remove physical blockages in your body or help you transmute negative energy into a positive force.

What Happens Next?

Once you have read about the karmic spaces in the chapters that follow, begin to observe yourself and see if you can recognize where you have become stuck.

At first, you may not notice karmic patterns except in hindsight. Or you may simply be aware that you are suffering mentally, but you aren't sure why. In that case, flip through the book until you find which space is at work. Your intuition will tell you.

To develop this awareness, you may want to journal about your experiences with the spaces, as noted in the "Practices" section. Make a list of any thoughts or emotions you remember having just *before* you became stuck in a karmic space. You may notice some of the following:

- You found yourself giving in to negative feelings—especially hopelessness or powerlessness.
- You noticed tension building in your body.
- Your mind was chattering with resentments, rationalizations, and self-justifications. (Just note them very briefly. Writing them in detail may only reinforce the karmic space or, worse, bring you back into it!)

When you are struggling with a karmic space, turn to the practices at the end of each chapter. All of the practices are gentle ways to distract the grip of your ego, which is holding you in the karmic space. As you try them out and learn them, you may find yourself turning to them more and more in the moment.

Once you notice that you can catch yourself falling into the karmic spaces, or even before you fall in, you'll get a feeling: I can do this. I can feel the aliveness that comes from being free. You begin to remember that you have choices. This is a very powerful process. As you free yourself from even a little bit of karma, the karmic connections loosen, the breath becomes freer, and you are more ready to explore the moment and all its joys.

To begin, close your eyes and breathe into your heart center in the middle of your chest, and ask yourself, Where am I stuck? If the answer comes to you, trust it. Don't second guess yourself. Intuition has spoken in your heart.

Choosing Freedom

All the karmic spaces hold us in the past or keep us focused on an imaginary future. Yet, your innate wisdom has a life of its own, ready to awaken and bring you into this moment.

Let it awaken! This you must do in order to go on with your life, to complete this life's puzzle. Otherwise, you'll be revisiting, revisiting, revisiting, your past. Or you'll be always looking ahead, living an imaginary life. The past is finished, the future is illusion, and you're right *here*.

Some have said that believing in karma leads to a kind of fatalism, or passivity, or helplessness. This is a huge misunderstanding. There is nothing passive about choosing to be free. Karma means action, and choosing freedom calls on us to act, to choose, and to take a different way.

The tools in this book can offer you ways to a freer, simpler, happier life. They can also start you on the road to liberation, *samadhi*, Christ consciousness, nirvana—whatever you call that state of alignment with something greater than your small self, that inner freedom the great mystics of every religion speak of.

Now ask yourself again: What do I really want?

Whatever the answer, let us begin.

PART TWO

The Karmic Spaces

CHAPTER THREE

Jealousy

Recognizing the Karmic Space

Jealousy interrupts the path to liberation.

D o you want what someone else has? Do you judge yourself for not having it? Do you swing back and forth between anger and regret? These are some of the signs that you are stuck in the karmic space of jealousy. In the space of jealousy, we focus on other people so much that we become obsessed with them. We may even begin to hate them. But then, through self-judgment and guilt, we turn those feelings on ourselves, and we engineer our own depression.

Like all karma, jealousy goes around in a self-reinforcing spiral. While you're busy looking at others, jealousy will awaken in you every other negative emotion. That's why jealousy often begins slowly and then suddenly bursts forth like an angry beast. The anger arises because someone has what you want and think you deserve. Your co-worker just got the job you wanted, and now you have to smile and congratulate him. Yet, you *know* you deserved that job. You remember all the projects you worked so hard on, but he seemed to get all the credit. Next you decide that he undermined you on purpose. Still, you have to pretend to be gracious, so you don't even allow yourself the luxury of saying nasty things about him.

Since there's nothing you can do about your co-worker, you may turn your anger against yourself: Why was I so clueless? I'm always being taken advantage of. On and on, you talk to yourself like that, and you may even talk yourself into depression. You blame yourself, you sink into the quicksand of self-pity, and maybe you find ways to punish yourself. Around you go, obsessing about past hurts, plotting revenge, hating yourself, fantasizing about quitting your stupid job. Meanwhile, your coworker has no idea of the drama you are creating in your mind about him!

To consistently project jealousy on others creates instantaneous karma; in other words, it hurts you more than it hurts them. As you're obsessing, you're inflicting "self-karma" upon yourself, and you pay for it almost instantly with the pain in the pit of your belly.

As long as you don't act on your jealousy, as long as it doesn't affect another human being, self-karma can dissipate on its own. However, when you hurt somebody else, that is karma you have to pay for. Jealousy becomes anger, next it becomes rage, and you strike out. Now the person you hurt starts taking his anger out on others, and you've started a chain reaction. From there, it's very, very hard to get out of that karma, extraordinarily hard. Jealousy gets wrapped around your neck until you can't even breathe.

You could lighten the pain just by acknowledging jealousy: "I was kind of jealous when you got the promotion, but you're doing a great job." It would not actually kill you to say this! Even though it may seem a little silly, it would ease your heart, until jealousy holds you less tightly in its grip.

WHO ARE YOU JEALOUS OF?

It is about you!

The truth of jealousy is that you aren't jealous of anybody else but yourself. You are probably aware of feelings of jealousy toward others, what you may be unaware of are your own feelings of unworthiness and disappointment in yourself. Instead of looking at yourself, you cling to jealousy, never pursuing what you want or need, looking at all the people who, so you think, have more than you do. That is the biggest illusion, the belief that your jealousy is about another person. In reality, you are jealous of yourself!

Aren't you the most jealous of people who have achieved *your* dream? If you never thought about being a singer, you're probably not jealous of the latest star, and if you never cared about sports, you're not jealous of someone on the winning team. If you never cared much about money, you're not jealous of some billionaire. Well, a little bit you are, but we are talking about the bitter jealousy that shrinks you down until your whole life is about clinging to the sides of the karmic cubbyhole until you're unable to move in any direction.

This karmic space is a kind of blindness, especially blindness to your own beauty. Wherever you are in your life, you have some abilities, some talents, but if you're stuck in jealousy you can't use them—you're too busy looking at others. Did you fail to write that song, patent that invention, build that house, follow that career, have the family you wanted—and then discover that *someone else went and did it?* Now you're not just jealous of yourself, you're angry at yourself too, because you see what other people are doing and you know you could have done it too.

It's possible to be jealous of yourself in the present, the future, or the past—who you are now, who you will become, even who you were. Yes, you can be jealous of who you were, if you have an impression of having been somehow greater in the past. This is when people look back with nostalgia. This kind of jealousy often comes as the feeling that your best days are behind you, or that life is passing you by. You can also be jealous of yourself in some imaginary present, the wonderful person you would be if only you weren't overweight, if only you hadn't married the wrong person, if only you hadn't lost all that money. You can also be jealous of your future self. You just know there is a wise and wonderful person inside of you waiting to burst forth someday! It's not karma to have an emotion that passes, like envy: "Oh, I want that!" Like all emotions, it comes and goes. To see the difference between envy and the karmic space of jealousy, ask yourself two things: First, would I hurt someone to get what he has? And second,

Would I hurt myself? If you're not hurting anyone, you may be able to transform a little jealousy into a positive movitation.

I grew up in a cellar apartment, but in a nice neighborhood, and it was obvious that others had more than I did. In the evening, I would look in the windows of all the houses where families were sitting down to dinner. Meanwhile, I was hanging out with the homeless people under the Boardwalk in Brighton Beach. They'd get food from the trash cans outside of Nathan's in Coney Island, yet they'd never complain. Anyway, that's what I envied—not the nice things people had, or the food, but the way they sat down to dinner together as a family. I wanted that and I dreamed that, if I ever had children, we would all sit down to dinner. So when I got married, I became a terrific cook. (If I weren't a spiritual teacher, I'd have my own cooking show on TV by now.) We had a great big table, and that's where I fed a lot of the neighborhood kids along with my own, because I knew what that could mean to a child.

But I didn't just cook—I ate, too. So I gained a few pounds. Now I was annoyed by skinny little girls like my first yoga teacher. She must have been a size zero! If I were a deeply jealous person, I might have said, "Oh, I want to kill her for being so skinny." But it's not true. I didn't want to hurt her, I was just dying to find out how she did it.

I'd heard it was yoga that makes you thin, and that's all I wanted. Even so, out of jealousy of the teacher, I almost walked right out of my first yoga class. Right there, you can see the difference between the passing emotion of envy and karmic jealousy, which hurts yourself or others. Karmic jealousy would have had me walk straight across the street to have a piece of cheesecake. Then I would never have learned anything.

Everybody has some jealousy, or some envy, but the difference is, I never wanted to hurt myself or anyone else to get what I wanted. I never wasted a lot of my time worrying about what I didn't have.

Karmic Connections

Always entwined with jealousy is the thought that your life isn't full. It's as though you are surrounded by cloudy mirrors so you just can't see your own beauty.

No karmic pattern exists in isolation. Every karmic space is connected to others. Recognizing these connections may make you feel as if wherever you turn you are stepping into a new trap. For jealousy, the connections that most often arise are obsession, judgment, guilt, and regret.

OBSESSION

You need not go forth on a battleground of ego,
for ego is truly just the chatter of the mind.

If you're obsessed with something, you're focused only on the negative, the lack of something, and you are putting great importance on what you lack instead of on what you have. If this describes you, then ask yourself, "Is it worth enough that I should let it crush my life?" Because that is what obsession does, crushes the life out of you.

Everybody has pain in their lives, but jealousy makes us dwell on our losses. Pain attracts more pain, it becomes a habit, it causes deep sadness, and finally it takes root as depression. We feel as if someone else, or something outside of us, controls us. If we cannot find happiness within ourselves, it must be outside, and we feel helpless when we can't find it.

If we look around outside ourselves, there is an endless supply of things to be jealous of. You may think, Oh, if I just had more money I'd be OK; I wouldn't want anything. Oh yes, you would. There would always be something else. You'd want to be beautiful, because you forget about your inner beauty. You'd wish you had a better personality. You'd want to be young again. You'd want to be famous.

But even the rich and famous, even lottery winners and movie stars, have problems. They get divorced, they get addicted, they gain weight, and you would know that if you just read *People* magazine like I do! The Buddha explained the endless nature of desire, but you can see what he meant just by watching television gossip shows. Look, you can even be jealous that your dog runs to someone else before you. It's the oldest story in the world, but it still catches us.

Why do we fall for it? Because when we are jealous we are out of the moment. We are in someone else's business, someone else's moment, and not our own. That's an easy place to hide, like all the karmic spaces.

There is a heaviness that comes from always looking to the future, always dwelling on what you don't have, always wondering when you will have that which another has. You can change these thoughts into a positive knowing, telling yourself, "It will come." You will eventually get what you want, although maybe not when you want it. Yes, in the abundance of the universe, you can actually achieve anything. Therefore, be sure you know what you truly want before you waste a life following someone else's dream. Quit focusing on what you lack and begin to find your own way.

JUDGMENT

Do not let your emotions turn you away from your Self.

We've all had the experience of judging someone, perhaps on a first impression, and then finding out we got it wrong. Even though we know our own judgments can be off, we tend to believe in or imagine the judgments of others and turn them into self-judgment. Self-judgment turns to unworthiness, the persistent feeling that you are just not good enough and never will be. You begin to feel that you don't even deserve whatever good comes your way.

When you feel jealous, remember that we can never know another's karma. No matter who you are jealous of or why, each person's story is unique. You can't know if you'd be willing to do what it took to achieve what anyone else has, at least not unless you're willing to live his life instead of your own. Remember for a moment the situation where your coworker got the job you wanted. In the big picture, do you want the pressures that come with that promotion? Would you exchange your life for his? You don't even know what he may have gone through, or what problems he faces right now. Would you really trade?

GUILT AND REGRET

Answers come from the moment.
Only questions come from the past.

Deep down, a part of you knows that you let yourself down. You say to yourself, I missed the boat, or I didn't grasp it, or I should have lost weight last year but it's hopeless now. I could have, should have, would have…. Guilt and regret, like fear, flow through all the karmic spaces.

Devoting yourself to jealousy is taking up all the energy that you might have spent on your next opportunity—the new job, the new lover, the next project. How often have you started something with high hopes, but it just didn't work out? Often, your dream fizzles out slowly, but something always stops you. This time, look closely until you can see the karmic pattern. Does the same thing stop you again and again? Is it fear of rejection or simply fear of failure? Many of us fear success even more than we fear failure, because failure is so familiar. Even if you try something new, you can create failure in a thousand subtle ways. The cycle continues, but it's stronger now because you know it could have been different. Often your response to failure is just more jealousy. But never in a million years will jealousy get you what you want.

Karmic Graces

Our habit of comparing ourselves to others has us believe that our own lives are at a standstill. But the truth is, our hearts are always able to move beyond our minds, which means that we can have expansion in any moment, simply by learning from our innate wisdom.

What you must know is that you too could achieve your dream. Most of the time it is yours already. You only need to dig deep enough within yourself to find it. Once you have even the slightest understanding of who you really are, then you can reclaim all the abilities that you stifled with jealousy. But this requires self-love and gratitude.

SELF-LOVE

Write the story of your life in pencil
so you can change the ending any time you want.

We all get caught in thinking we have to prove something to somebody, but of course this is an illusion. Who do you think is keeping score? Universal spirit loves us unconditionally, just as we are. Since everyone has a perfect soul, none greater, none lesser, there's nothing to prove. When we are in the karmic space of jealousy, however, we may recognize this light in others, but we only want to shoot it down and make it disappear. Instead, we can learn to look for the true Self in all beings. The true Self is love. Where there is so much love, how can there be jealousy?

When you are struggling with jealousy, sit quietly and feel the universe unfold in your heart. Truly, there is no difference between opening to universal love and beginning to love yourself. Go deeply into your heart, and you will see that you have the light, you have everything you need for happiness within yourself. You have no need to be eaten up by jealousy. When you remember your own beautiful heart, then you will be willing to let others have what they have without resenting them, for you are comfortable and secure in knowing that you are loved.

Self-love brings the confidence to go after your dreams. Gradually you can begin to be aware when jealousy starts to hit you. You can fall in love with your own moment, and you will begin to understand when jealousy takes you away from it. That's when you say the magic word, "STOP," and come back to your Self.

A STUDENT'S STORY: MY WHITE PICKET FENCE

I was having dinner with a group of colleagues as they were discussing their spouses, children, home renovations, and vacation plans, all sounding quite cozy and intimate. One of them turned to me and innocently asked whether I had children, and then whether I was married. I felt like I was being put on the spot. A heavy, toxic darkness intruded on my simple state of being as I stumbled through a response that would take the spotlight off of me as quickly as possible so I could avoid feeling judged for being the only single, childless person at the table.

I love being single and am generally quite content to be traveling independently through life. I am fulfilled by my work, hobbies, friends, family, and community. Yet it's taken me a long time to be able to trust that it's OK to be single. My mind starts comparing my life to those of people in relationships. Impressions from the media, romance novels, fairy tales and such infect my mind with self-doubt. Being single must mean that I should feel lonely, unloved, and incomplete. I compare myself to those who appear to be living that blissful "white picket fence" life and … in creeps jealousy.

It's getting easier to catch myself, label those thoughts as jealousy, then let them go without judging myself or anyone

(continues)

else. It's great to recognize that what I felt jealous of at the table that day was just the sense of belonging and bonding being expressed by the others. I have my own unique and wonderful life, so what I thought I was jealous of was actually just a temporary sense of disconnection from something I have had all along.

GRATITUDE

A grateful heart can consume the karma of all lifetimes.

The greatest key to the karmic space of jealousy is gratitude. Even though gratitude is easily lost in the fog of the mind, you can make a conscious practice of it. Gratitude is a practice of renewal, taking you way beyond self-pity, tiredness, guilt, anger, beyond all the little shards that jealousy puts in your heart.

Ingratitude has you go back in time to collect all the pain you've ever felt, all the wrong choices you've ever made, and then it bursts forth carrying all this negativity into the now. There's always something to complain about, but when you constantly complain, you fall so far down into a black hole that only gratitude can lift you out. "But," you say, "there's so much pain in the world …." Or you say, "My life is such a mess, so where do I even begin to be grateful?" Don't waste time on all that, even if it's true. Just begin to unravel your karma.

Just say, "Thank you." If you don't believe in God, thank nature, or thank yourself. It is the inner movement of gratitude that matters, not who you say it to. That means really looking at your life. Thank you for what? Think of three things right now, three things you are grateful for. Even if you have to fake it, come up with just three things. Maybe it's, Thank you for my health. If you're not so healthy, you're still breathing, so, Thank you for my breath. If you're fighting an illness, have gratitude for every day, every second. If you're fighting depression, realize that gratitude and depression cannot live in the same moment. Suddenly you can't think of three things, not because there's nothing to be grateful for, but because there are so many things! Now would be a good time to start a gratitude book, just a place where you write a few things each day that you are grateful for. This seems simple, but it's a powerful practice that can change your whole outlook.

Eventually the moment comes when you become so grateful that the light shines right through every lifetime and brings you to this moment. In spite of all the pain you've ever felt, you realize, This very moment brings me to this space of gratitude. And therefore I am. Therefore I am! It is a space of deep stillness. This stillness has no religion. This stillness has no name. It comes from the left, it comes from the right, and explodes in the heart. And this is how we welcome ourselves. We realize we are complete, so complete that we need nothing even while the possibilities exist for us to have everything. In this space, there is no room for jealousy.

Practices for Letting Go

Knowing how jealousy confines you, your whole life begins to change. You can quit looking outside yourself, you can begin to look for happiness within, and jealousy will begin to melt away in the fire of awareness. You can think of the practices that follow as preparation. The next time jealousy comes toward you, you will be ready for it.

JOURNAL: DOES IT FIT?

Desire for possession poisons the heart space.

In your journal, write five things that other people have, things you want so badly that it makes you jealous. Go ahead, make it specific—not just "a new car," but "Dr. Kantor's new BMW convertible," because you spotted it outside her office and you thought to yourself, So that's where my money goes.

When we were younger we were able to pretend and fantasize all the time, so go ahead, imagine you have it. Once you are riding around in it, ask yourself: Do I like the color? Did I want leather seats? Maybe I should have gotten the windows tinted. Then ask, Do I even like this car? How much, on a scale of one to ten? Now you can wonder, Does it fit my life? Finally ask, Do I even need it?

Do this exercise for five things or five people, listing what you're jealous of and then imagining you have all of it. By asking, Does it fit? about each one, you'll be surprised how often the answer is, No, not really; it doesn't fit.

If you discover, No, I don't really want that, now you know that the ego mind was using jealousy to distract you from happiness, and you can stop dwelling on it. But if you do want this car or whatever it is, you can begin to inquire into what is stopping you, and you can work toward it without confusion.

VISUALIZATION: A PILGRIMAGE

The real journey is in your heart.

What if you considered life as a form of divine pilgrimage? In any moment or even before prayer or meditation, imagine that you are on your pilgrimage. Think of three things you would not carry with you, such as obsession, judgment, and guilt. That bundle is heavy! Lay it down. Touch your heart with your right hand and say, "Obsession, I leave you and you cannot follow me." If you do this, you will begin to feel lighter and lighter.

Think of your judgments. Can you leave them behind? How about guilt? That's another heavy one. For each burden, acknowledge it, say goodbye to it, and leave it behind you. (Don't worry, you can always go back and pick them up later, if you really want to.)

Close your eyes, and feel where you are inside.

MEDITATION: JUST A THOUGHT

Your thoughts have no roots. Let them go.

Negative thinking pulls you out of the moment, and once you are out of the moment you are further and further away from the soul. Yet negativity can become a habit, and negative thoughts can compound themselves until they feel very real.

Sitting in meditation, or just walking through your day, begin to notice your negative thoughts, starting with the familiar thoughts of envy, anger, resentment, and regret that fuel the space of jealousy. When thoughts come, say to yourself, It's just a thought, and let the thought go, again and again and again. Don't fight a thought, don't analyze it, don't try to stop it, and above all, don't fall into the trap of thinking like this: I'm too negative all the time. I'll never get this. Why am I so bad at meditation? Those are just thoughts too.

When you get a little space between thoughts, ask yourself, I wonder what my next thought will be? This confuses the ego mind so much that it gives you a chance to feel your true Self.

CHAPTER FOUR

Anger

Recognizing the Karmic Space

Anger steals the stillness of the soul.

Did you ever get so angry that you just couldn't stop your mouth, so you kept hurting another person more and more? When we are angry, we know we're doing something wrong, but we don't know how to stop ourselves, and we keep it going. This kind of experience reveals how powerful the karmic space of anger can be.

Sometimes people ask me, "Was I born angry?" and the answer is no. You were born perfect. Later your *samskaras*, your old karmic patterns, shaped how you reacted when you found yourself in an imperfect world. For many, anger comes from seeking and not finding. When children don't find answers as they grow up, they start to look to drugs or alcohol, anything to escape from a world that is void of spirituality. Pay attention to the questions your children ask you: "How did I get here?" "What is behind the sky?" "Where did my dog go when he died?" These are the questions that ignite a child's mind, for they are really spiritual questions.

There are always consequences with anger, whether we project it out onto others, or in on ourselves. If you cling to anger and hold it in, you can't breathe deeply, because if you breathe deeply you'll have to think deeply, and if you think deeply, you'll have to think of whatever hurt you. Soon there's no breath for life. Your anger will solidify into a heavy cemented anger.

When you have an angry reaction over anything big or small, expressed or not, you open up new grooves within yourself. You deepen these grooves every time you have another angry reaction. This is karmic anger. It keeps pulling you back, keeps you running and running in the same old track.

MANY ANGERS

Anger takes up five times as much space as love.

Anger takes many forms, and the karmic space of anger has many small spaces within it. Blame, shame, hurt, and guilt all live close to anger, and so do fear, paranoia and revenge.

Anger easily mixes itself into righteousness, and so there are always bigots who, in their own anger, go after everyone and anyone who is different or unique. When another person's anger comes at you, it can awaken your feelings of shame, which many of us first learned in childhood just by absorbing the judgments of others. Shame takes infinite forms, and anger mixed with shame can develop into feelings of unworthiness, so that you are constantly saying you're sorry. You let your shoulders sag with burdens that do not even exist. Now the slightest perceived criticism can cause you to go to a deep place of depression or even false anger—false because you misperceived what was really said.

False anger mixes with fear and becomes paranoia. Now you may feel you must attack first before you are attacked. Then there is rage, which comes after anger has succeeded in spreading to your blood stream and stealing some beats of your heart. Rage literally burns up your life force and wastes it. An angry person's temperature goes up. So does the blood pressure, and everything is forgotten in the moment, except anger.

There are many kinds of anger, and they all feed each other in a karmic cycle. There may seem to be no way out. If we go around expressing anger and starting fights, we only create more anger.

Yet if we fear our own anger, if we can't express it properly, we are left with shame and guilt, and so around we go again and again.

Anger creates its own prison bars, and we can only look out between them. This is the story of all the karmic spaces: You place yourself in prison and you hold the key to the lock. You refuse to use it because you will have to admit that you have a way out.

Karmic Connections

There are many reasons for anger, and many triggers, but all have one thing in common: Whether he is angry at God, or the world, or himself, an angry person has forgotten his true nature. He has forgotten that everything we seek is right here, inside us. Forgetting this, we may do the same things over and over until we are worn out completely by the world. There are many karmic connections to anger. Among them are deliberate anger, anger at injustice, anger at God, and revenge.

DELIBERATE ANGER

Sometimes you think you are being hurt,
when in reality it is only your ego being hurt.

Often anger begins in fear. A mother sees her child almost get hit by a car, and she is terrified. But the child isn't hurt, and the car goes on down the street. That huge breath she took has to go somewhere, so suddenly she is screaming at her child, raging like crazy, and the poor kid has no clue. He doesn't realize that the rage coming toward him began in a mother's love.

Sometimes we get angry and we don't know why. Sometimes what we are angry about just seems stupid, even to us. For example, it could be the fly batting your window pane that is driving you crazy. You just get angrier and angrier, because you're using that anger to cover up something else.

THE 11 KARMIC SPACES

You can let anger go if you can acknowledge it: "Wow, I'm really angry." Or you can question it, "Am I really feeling hurt?" When you can differentiate between anger and hurt, then you can let both go. When we are hurt, we're open, and the heart feels soft and vulnerable. When we're angry, we're in a defensive place, and the heart closes. That's when the anger is a tool to mask the hurt.

So anger can begin as another emotion, including fear and hurt. No matter where it begins, it becomes "deliberate anger" when you reach for things to be angry about. You wrap yourself in it when you feel vulnerable—when you are afraid, or hurt, or ashamed. I have heard, "You can hang your soul on the hook of anger and it will stay warm." Maybe so, but the heat of anger is a false warmth, a false comfort.

It's not all that different from picking up a drink or a drug to hide our weakness. For example, you're worried about losing your job, or you're worried about the mortgage, and you come home to find your kids have left a mess in the living room. We all know what can happen next, but why? Psychologists might call this anger "displacement" because you are yelling at your children instead of the bank. I call it deliberate anger simply because you made a choice when you opened your mouth to yell.

ANGER AT INJUSTICE

The heart does not have questions and answers, it just is.

It is easy for a spiritual teacher to say, "Give up anger." There is reason for anger if we look at the plight of the world's children—and I don't just mean the babies, I mean all Earth's children who are caught in war, hunger, disease, injustice. Sometimes it looks as if there's no justice anywhere in the world.

Among my students are mothers who have lost their children or whose children are terribly sick. Of course they are angry at times. There is no point in denying it because that would only lead to resignation and depression. There are certain times when the anger has to boil in order to be cleaned out. But in a quiet moment I ask them, "At this point, will anger hinder your life?" It's not about right and wrong, justice or injustice, it's just that holding onto anger is not going to help them or their children in any way. There is enough injustice in the world that we could be angry all the time, and who would that help?

It is possible to live with a heart that is passionate about injustice, though this can resemble anger. Confusion comes when you mix your personal anger in with your passion for justice. Then, no matter how hard you work for your ideals, little is being accomplished except your own bondage.

ANGER AT GOD

God cries with you.

People always want to know, "How could God let this happen?" There is no reason for a lot of terrible things that happen, no reason whatsoever. But this question can make us feel vulnerable and afraid, then angry. So you have to learn what to do with this anger, what do with this pain.

Growing up, I'd wander the streets of Coney Island and sometimes hang out under the Boardwalk. There I saw real pain, homeless men and women who lived there, dying early and in pain because of drink, drugs, loneliness. I understood then what true anger is—that it comes from a deep place in the heart.

At night I would sit with them by the trash can fire, they with their drink and me with a net that I used to hold the coins that fell through the cracks in the boardwalk. As the night got longer and my people got drunker or more stoned, their anger would come. Sometimes I became afraid—not that they would hurt me, but afraid because I thought, What if they never find what they need? What if they never get what they are asking for? What if they will never be out of pain?

My friend and protector was Big Henry. His wife and children had been killed by a drunk driver on Ocean Parkway. Where was God to allow that to happen? Henry never blamed the drunk driver, who was just a kid really, but he was terribly angry at God.

So now, if someone asks me Big Henry's questions, I tell them the truth: I don't know why this happened or that happened. What I do know, deep in my heart, is that when you're crying, God is crying with you, and you're never alone. God didn't reach out to hurt you. It's not about justice, and it's not about those children's karma or Big Henry's karma. Somebody chose to have a few drinks and steal a car and take a wrong turn, and there was Big Henry's family right in the way. So it's all choice, our human choice, and one choice can start a whole karmic chain. How else can it make any sense—a family just wanting to enjoy a day at the beach and a drunk driver smashes into them?

I think of Big Henry when I see those who are angry at God. What I've found is that the only way to stop the flow of this very messy energy is to serve and take care of people. Henry had lost his whole family, and mine wasn't doing a great job of raising me, so we kind of found each other. Despite his anger and pain, Big Henry gave me love. When you reach out to help someone, the anger just falls away because you are using it. You are putting anger to use in the name of that same God you are angry with.

REVENGE

God's time is not the same as ours.

In the space that anger creates in your heart, waves of thoughts of revenge come and go easily. There's nothing like plotting revenge—it can be delicious. But, though revenge may ease your pain in the moment, like all instant gratification, it doesn't last long before you need it again and again.

Thoughts carry their own karma. When you have a revenge thought and you act on it, then it is double-bad karma, the thought and the action. Yet when you have such a thought and you do not act, then you consume the thought and the action. That can equal good karma.

The real danger in indulging in thoughts of revenge is that they may lead to action. Revenge is the essence of reaction. The cycle continues, and karma solidifies. What good is it to kill a human being for the crime of killing a human being? What good is it to go to war and strike out against people whose families will seek revenge and eventually strike out against your country or you? Taking revenge on any human being, country, or group of people is never justified, and, in terms of karma, revenge makes absolutely no sense whatsoever.

If you believe in reincarnation, just imagine what happens if we take our anger with us into death. We may return next life with a desire to seek revenge, if we can just figure out whom we have sworn vengeance toward. Or we may not even call it revenge—we may call it justice. So we go through life looking for something to be angry about, and of course we find it. Sometimes we'll take a slight hurt and magnify it, just because our karmic attitude of revenge must find a target somewhere. You don't even have to believe in reincarnation to see how this works. We carry anger from moment to moment, year to year, and from lifetime to lifetime, even as memory fades.

You probably won't use the word revenge, but isn't that what you want when you fantasize that the laws of karma will settle the score for you? You think, I want to be there when his karma catches up with him—and the sooner the better. You want revenge now. But the law of karma isn't about revenge or retribution, it just is. Karma is a law of nature like gravity. Karma plays itself out, but not on our petty timetables. You have to have some faith in yourself and in the way of things and not insist that all karma be acted out immediately, or even in this lifetime. Eventually, all karma becomes a perfectly balanced equation.

Sometimes we want the universe to take revenge for us, so we imagine a vengeful God. Some religions even promote revenge as a pathway to liberation. But I wouldn't call that either religion or liberation. A religion is supposed to be a group of people that worship God together. I don't know a God that cries out for blood, I don't know a vengeful God, and I don't know a judgmental God.

"An eye for an eye makes the whole world blind," said Gandhi. Martin Luther King said it too, and they both based it on Christ's teaching to turn the other cheek. Why would you let revenge blind you?

Karmic Graces

The key to unraveling every karmic space is to listen to your heart before you do again what you have been doing for all your life, or even lifetimes. When you give up anger, you finally discover your true strength. The greatest keys to getting out of the karmic space of anger are non-reaction and forgiveness.

NON-REACTION

To let anyone lead you into anger
is to give up a piece of your heart.

Someone around you is angry. Do you really want to step into that? If you react to someone who is spitting her pain out at you, not only are you causing yourself pain, but you've moved right into that person's life. You're reacting to things in "her" life, things you don't even understand, can't understand. You don't know what happened in her life, or childhood, or even what happened today to put her in this state, but if you're reacting, then you're involved. You're mixing your karma with hers. This is an example of a double karmic boundary: what happens when you get involved with another person in any negative way. We see this most often with anger.

If you stay aware, every interaction is an opportunity for growth. So the next time you feel yourself being drawn into someone else's anger, say to yourself, Stop! This is the simple practice of hesitation, of not reacting for just one moment. In the beginning, this will take some will power. You may find it hard to hold your tongue because you have such interesting things to say, and so many clever comebacks are buzzing around in your brain.

Stop! Learn to soften your thoughts before you speak them. Notice your breath and soften the breath around your heart. Awaken your inner core of love—it is still there, even when you forget it. Even if you have to struggle not to say angry words, even if you feel like a hypocrite, the struggle will be worth every effort to win. After a while the mind begins to listen to the heart and becomes more balanced. It only takes a split second in time and space, and in that split second your essential nature will kick in and your lips will not form those words of anger.

A STUDENT'S STORY: THE DISH PIG

It's a cold morning and I pop out of bed, hopeful and looking forward to getting some writing in before everyone wakes up. I walk out into the kitchen to make my tea, and there before me is a mess. Sharing a house with others, it's often nice to have a community, but really, who wants to wake up to an overflowing dish drainer, dirty dishes, sticky counters, and a stove with spilled, burnt-on gunk? My happy mood flies out the window. I decide to just make some tea and toast and work around the mess rather than confront it. While waiting for the water to boil, I stare angrily out the window. "No, I will NOT touch that mess! They just do this because they know I'll clean up after them." I no sooner get the tea made than another

(continues)

resident comes and plunks his stuff down right in front of the toaster.

"Are you going to be long?" I huff out, clearly not meaning to be pleasant.

"Oh, were you going to make something? I can move."

"Not now," I say gathering up my tea (still no toast). I go stomping off into my room.

I am in such a foul mood. How blind can one person be? I was clearly going to make toast. Why does he always have to use all three counters to make his breakfast anyway? I am so tired of these men thinking they're entitled to be waited on hand and foot.

My mind is spiraling out of control with negativity approaching straight venom. Then I think, "Oh, just STOP!" I don't want to behave like this anymore. STOP. It takes a few minutes, but the steam begins to stop coming out of my ears.

I head back into the kitchen a few minutes later and say, "I didn't mean to bark at you. I was in a bad mood. Sorry." He gives me a hug, and then I notice the dishes have all been put away! I've been working on anger for a long time, but that day I got the upper hand. It felt pretty good, and next time I'll catch it sooner.

FORGIVENESS

One forgives in order to rejoin the flow of life.

People say they forgive, especially when the cameras are rolling. But in reality, if you knew you could get away with hurting the person who killed your child, would you do it?

Sometimes people really try to forgive, but then they live in a shadow of doubt, and the thought lingers, Maybe I didn't love her as much as I thought. It feels as if giving up your anger means you're giving up your child.

As with karma, each story is individual, unique. Forgiveness is not like a big spiritual epiphany. It happens slowly, after many, many days and nights of horrendous pain, many thoughts of revenge, many nights struggling with the question *why*. Whole lifetimes are lived in between the harm done and the forgiveness.

Does forgiveness break the karmic chain of anger? Not exactly. Each person has his own karma to play out. Forgiveness just allows you to step out to the side, step out of the cycle. I wouldn't tell you to go to the person who killed your child and say, "I forgive you." But you could start at the edges. Can you forgive the person who let him drive drunk? Can you forgive whoever gave him his first drink? Start like that and go very slowly. When you can, imagine coming face to face with him. Will anything raise your child from the dead? Do you truly want the revenge of another death, with his mother grieving the same as you? Forgiveness just takes one beat of a heart, one unconditional leap. Every single time you forgive, even for a split second, there is a very, very short lapse of a memory gone into love.

Forgiveness takes lifetimes.

Forgiveness happens in a split second.

Both are true. Thoughts of revenge will come again and again, but you can learn to look for the moments of forgiveness that come to you.

As you forgive, do you forget? I have many students who have come to me with tales of abuse, horrendous things they suffered in childhood, and even if it is buried deep within them, the pain is still there. Often they can't love themselves, but if they can't love themselves, they can't forgive. And if they can't forgive, they can't love themselves. The cycle goes around both ways. So I tell them, forgive but never forget.

Remember, but don't act and don't react, not even in your thoughts. There it is again, the power of hesitation and non-reaction to break the chains of karma by breaking the chain of cause and effect. If you have one angry thought about one person that you hate, one person you dislike, or even if there's someone who constantly annoys you, see if that person can be used for your own heart to grow.

Over the years, I've worked with children who have been terribly abused. One day, I was asked if I would work with a group of parents. I said, "Of course," without quite realizing what was being asked of me.

I walked into a room with a bunch of people. Everyone was wearing name tags with two names on them, a child's and the parent's. That's when it hit me: There was Johnny's mother. I had just held Johnny in my arms while he cried for the mother who had abused him. Then in came a whole group of men in handcuffs and chains, right off a prison bus, and I got it—these people were the abusers.

I'd never really experienced hate, but I hated what these people had done to those children. I couldn't even raise my eyes to look at them. I don't know how long we sat like that, until I recognized it: This is what hate feels like, I thought, and I realized that, if I get stuck in hate, I will never again be able to help another person.

So I lifted my eyes from the floor, and I really looked at them. Each one of them became a child to me. I saw how each one of them had also suffered in childhood. I had no right to judge, and that meant I had no right to forgive. Finally I asked them, these child abusers, to forgive me for my blindness.

Some of them were there just to get points off their jail time, but some were touched, and a few truly realized what they had done. Did it matter? They were still in jail, and their children would go on suffering. But, no matter what you have done, if you feel even the slightest amount of remorse, then you have a future. Perhaps not this lifetime, but eventually some lifetime.

The power to forgive is not ours. It belongs to God. But we can embrace each other.

Practices for Letting Go

Anger is like fire, often a destructive force. Yet fire is also a symbol for transformation. We speak of the fire of intuition, the inner fire of the seat of power in the belly, and the sacrificial flame used in ceremonies the world over. Offer your burdens to the fire; the greater they are, the greater the possibility of transformation.

BREATH: THE INNER FIRE

When you absorb life whole, then everything is fuel.

You have an inner fire that can be fanned with your breath. Sit quietly, and begin the fire breath, by contracting your abdominal muscles quite quickly, over and over. Focus on pushing out the breath, and let the in breath take care of itself. Keep the breath in the belly, or the abdomen. As you breathe, fanning the inner fire, visualize the flame in the belly. Think of your anger, jealousy, pride, whatever you don't need. See it going into the fire. Talk to the flame: "Take this anger." As you allow negativity to burn, it becomes fuel. Like the Phoenix, you rise from the fire, up through the chakras toward higher consciousness, greater awareness, greater freedom. Your pain becomes fuel for the journey.

Don't strain. Just 30 seconds of fire breath is difficult if you're not used to it. Be careful and listen to your body. And check with your doctor before you do any kind of breath practice, especially if you are pregnant or have a health condition.

You are using the breath to awaken the power of the third chakra, so remember that power without love is nothing. The third chakra is the seat of power, but the fourth chakra, the heart, is the seat of love. No matter where your meditations or spiritual exercises take you, always use the awareness of breath to return to the heart. Breathe slowly for a few minutes, focusing your awareness in the center of your chest, and feel the gentle warmth that spreads around your heart as your anger eases.

ACTION: TRANSFORM EMOTIONS

One must move the body to understand the soul.

This short series lets us practice using hesitation to turn anger into compassion.

Begin in a kneeling or sitting position. Your hands are in tight fists. Inhaling deeply, extend your arms straight out to the sides at shoulder level. Now, exhale and, with all the force of rage, sweep your arms together in front of you so the sides of your fists are coming together, but STOP! Don't actually slam your fists together. Leave about an inch of space between your hands. Pause, then gently touch your fists together while holding the breath out.

Again, breathe in while you extend your arms out to the side again at shoulder level, still with tight fists. Now on a strong out breath swing your arms downwards in front of your hips. Stop. Pause. Touch fists, then return your arms to shoulder, keeping your fists together.

Finally, from the same starting position, sweep your arms upwards above your head. Stop. Pause. Touch. And once more behind you. Stop. Pause. Touch.

Repeat this sequence again, so that you have done eight sweeps in all, or two at each level. It's a powerful movement, made even more so because it ends with hesitation and a gentle touch.

ACTION: FIRE CEREMONY

The mind is in constant transformation.

The Self is always the same.

In every tradition there is fire, or an image of fire, to burn what you do not need.

You can make up your own fire ceremony, absolutely, as long as you are sincere and don't burn the house down. Think about the Wiccans, who have reinvented a ceremonial tradition that was brutally suppressed over centuries. They're not just making it up, they're drawing it from the universe; you can too, whether or not you have a specific tradition behind you. Make it simple or make it elaborate, do it alone or do it with others—just do what feels right to you.

Choose a special place for your fire, and make sure it is safe. Make it beautiful, and gather clean wood. You can say a prayer or invocation as you light the flame. Meanwhile, you have written on a piece of paper what you want to give up—one thing or many. Offer what you don't need. When the flame gets going, hold that paper to your heart, really visualize what you want to give up, and then throw it in, saying, "Take from me...." Stay there, watch everything burn to ash, and feel how quiet your heart can be.

CHAPTER FIVE

Pride

Recognizing the Karmic Space

You can listen to your ego or you can listen to your spirit.

Pride has a two-sided razor edge. The karmic space of pride keeps telling you one of two things at any given moment: one, that you are the most important person in the world, and two, that you are nothing at all. Pride never takes the middle path.

Like many of the karmic spaces, pride is rooted in fear, especially the fear of rejection. The ego wants you to think that your whole life is filled with mistakes, so it brings fear. Because we fear failure, we abandon our creative spirit and stop growing. Because we also fear success, we hide our abilities. No matter the reason for fear, we easily turn to the karmic space of pride. Sadly, often when we face an opportunity for happiness, we hide behind pride to cover our fear of disappointment.

You can follow pride down the path of unworthiness, feeling that whatever you do is just somehow not good enough. Or you can take the path of arrogance, thinking that you must be superior, and that's why people can't understand you.

Pride can take many forms, but it often leads people to veer back and forth between unworthiness and arrogance, leaving them terribly confused. They ask themselves: Am I really the worst person in the world and, if so, should I keep quiet and maybe hide under the bed? Or, am I really superior to others and, if so, should run for office or plan the perfect crime—whatever it takes to make sure I'm recognized for my brilliance?

ISOLATION

The true Self is always calling to you.
It is you that chooses not to hear.

On whatever path you take, even the one where you surround yourself with admirers and yes-men, you are alone with your pride. In this isolation the mind turns in on itself. Going further, you may become paranoid and think others are taking advantage of you. You begin to keep secrets. You pretend nothing bothers you, or else you take offense too easily. Blaming others, you rarely take responsibility for your own actions. You're always either playing "poor me," or else you're giving orders.

The illusions reinforce each other. The more you let the space of pride catch you, the more you cannot look beyond that space. When you swing toward arrogance, you can get caught in a different karmic space, the desire to be right. Until you are awakened from the illusion of pride, your mistakes can't teach you anything. There is nothing for you to learn, because you don't want to learn. When you swing toward unworthiness, you begin to think of your life as a dark place and, since you trust no one, you can't imagine that help is possible. You tell yourself, If there is no hope in my life, then let me pretend not to care. When you put a shield of pride in front of your eyes, you won't even notice if some light does come into your life.

As we become aware of the karmic spaces, pride is among the last to go, because it holds us in every other karmic space. If we're angry, pride says, "I'm not saying I'm sorry to that jerk." If we're jealous, pride says, "What do I have to be jealous of?" So then we don't learn what we need. Anger, at times, can be very cold, but pride is very hot. It actually hurts, deep in the heart, like a burning coal. That's the isolation of pride. It's too hot to carry around, but we *do* carry it, because we're too proud to put it down.

Karmic Connections

Although unworthiness and arrogance can be found in many of the karmic spaces, they are especially powerful when we are in the karmic space of pride. And sometimes the karmic connection appears as spiritual pride.

UNWORTHINESS

Dare to understand your own divine truth.

When you feel unworthiness, you don't believe you deserve the love that is available to you. Or you doubt your abilities so much that you never try to use them, and your gifts go to waste. Or you just assume that people think badly of you, so you don't make many friends. In unworthiness, a negative thought won't let you go, and you can't let it go. You wave to someone across a crowded room, and he ignores you. It's like you are nothing, just dirt under his shoe. You can't stop thinking about it. Maybe you find out later that his mother just died or he's about to lose his job. Or he lost his contact lenses and he didn't even see you. Before you learn the truth (and it could be years, or never), you just torment yourself.

Like anyone who works with people, I have to be careful that my words aren't taken the wrong way. I once told a student, "You are one of the purest people I know." She thought I said, "You're the most impure person I know." It took her ten years to ask me why I had said that; she had held it in all that time because unworthiness kept her from just asking.

Once you discover that you have been seeing your life through glasses clouded by unworthiness, you may ask, What else do I get wrong? You might be surprised at how much unworthiness colors everything you do.

ARROGANCE

Pride keeps pushing love away.

Arrogance develops from deep-rooted fear that somebody is going to see who you truly are, which is nothing. You hide your feeling of worthlessness behind arrogance. Feeling that you are less than others, you act like you're superior. You'd rather have people say about you, "He's very arrogant" instead of "He's just no good." You distract people and get them to focus on something other than the terrible emptiness you feel. It's all a cover-up.

You may tell yourself that your arrogance is confidence, but the only person you are fooling is yourself. Maybe what you really think is that you're sinful, or you have horrible karma, but more frightening is the feeling that you are *nothing*, or that there's just something wrong about you and you don't know what it is. Now you are back to the unworthiness part of the cycle. If somebody compliments you, if somebody loves you, you don't even know what to do with it.

SPIRITUAL PRIDE

Your strength is in your heart.
Your weaknesses are in your mind.

Chogyam Trungpa Rinpoche warned us, "Ego is constantly attempting to acquire and apply the techniques of spirituality for its own benefit." Spiritual pride is where unworthiness and arrogance come together in the pretense of spirituality.

When I was first teaching, I was under the wing of Hilda Charleton, who had a lot of students in New York. She told me about one boy who she said was going into samadhi, which is a very high state of consciousness. In some stages of samadhi, the yogi seems to leave the body completely and be absorbed into God consciousness. Hilda had spent many years in the spiritual centers of India, so this didn't strike her as all that unusual. So she invited this young man to meet me.

He showed up dressed all in white, with flowers and fruit to offer, the whole bit. Back then during the hippie era, a lot of my students were kind of scruffy looking, to tell the truth. It drove me crazy how they walked around Manhattan dressed in skeevy old blankets trying to look like they'd just come from a cave in the Himalayas. Now here arrived this "super yogi," all bright and shiny. The light just poured from him! The funny thing was, he was completely faking it, yet the light was real. I could have just enjoyed the show, but part of being a spiritual teacher is that you have to be ready to call people on their games.

A STUDENT'S STORY:
BEHIND THE CURTAIN

I had been doing my best to impress Hilda, and she had invited me to meet Ma. I was thinking, "I have one shot to make my mark. I'll go into samadhi, and she will love me." That's really all I wanted, to be loved, because I had such deep unworthiness. I had no idea what samadhi was, but I had heard stories of yogis who went stiff and didn't breathe, and I had faked it pretty well so far.

So I went to meet her at this gorgeous penthouse on Central Park West where she taught sometimes. Ma asked Hilda, "Where's the young man who's in samadhi?" She had me sit in front of her, told me to relax and shut my eyes, and she touched me on the forehead. I sat stiff as a board trying not to breathe. Actually, I was breathing very sneaky in and out of the side of my mouth. Meanwhile, I was going deeper and deeper into meditation because that's what happens when you sit in front of

(continues)

a master. After a while, I heard Ma say to Hilda, "Bring him down and give him some milk and cookies."

Oh wow, they love me! I'm really *in*! Hilda touched me, and I came out of meditation, had some milk and cookies, and went home. That night, Hilda called me: "I have a message from Ma." Now I get messages! I *am* special!

Hilda was always very prim and proper, so it was a shock to hear her repeating Ma's message straight from Brooklyn: "Don't ____ with me, I'm for real!" In fact she said it twice. "But you're welcome to come back on Thursday."

Why would I go back? But I did. I felt like I had to. This time I wore ordinary clothes. The room had heavy velvet floor-to-ceiling drapes, and I hid between the curtains and a window. Ma came in. Right away she said, "Where are you? I know you're here!" Then I had this terrible moment when I couldn't find my way out of the curtains. But there was no place to hide. She proceeded to tell me very specifically everything that was wrong with me. They say the ego has to die, and mine was on life support. But I kept going back. It was another two years before she spoke to me again. But that was the lesson—you don't have to impress anybody, you just have to be yourself.

Karmic Graces

The karmic spaces are not just about being stuck. They are a learning tool. With practice you will get to the point where you take two or three steps into pride, yet you will feel that gust of wind saying, "Be aware." Just by thinking that, you have practiced hesitation, you have broken a link in the chain of reaction, or you have unraveled another thread of karma. The isolation of pride can be broken in many ways, such as offering someone dignity, having humility or humor, and sharing.

DIGNITY

Treat others with dignity,
and you will find dignity within yourself.

A young man was trying to help his aging father with chores around the house, but the old man would just get angry. When he asked me what to do, I told him he would have to honor his father's pride. "Sit at the kitchen table and ask him to help you with a problem. Make up a problem if you have to, but you can't steal that pride from him. Then, as you talk, start with the kitchen, and wash a few dishes. Just get his mind off the fact that you are cleaning for him."

This question of dignity comes up a lot when you're working with the sick, the poor, the dying. I remember Crystal, who had lost four babies to AIDS. She was a prostitute and a drug addict, and she was dying. When she had only a few days left, she asked for her nails to be done, bright blue with little rhinestone stars on them. Maybe she was afraid I judged her for it because she explained, "Wherever I'm going, I want my babies to know me, I want them to find me." Holding up her beautiful nails to me, she said, "And now they'll recognize me."

Pride takes many forms, not always bad.

HUMILITY

Forged in the heat of compassion,
humility can only lead to strength.

Many of us feel that we need to be tough to face life and that being humble is a form of weakness. Pride, it turns out, is the real weakness. Humility is the karmic grace that develops naturally as we conquer pride. Humility takes many forms, just like pride. One kind of humility is when you ask for help with an open heart, an open mind, and an open soul, and you are willing to admit, I cannot help myself, and I need help. You could be speaking to a friend, a counselor, or to God in prayer, but no matter who you ask, you break a hole in the wall of pride. Does this sound like the beginning of a 12-step program? It is similar, and I have advised many people to try 12-step programs over the years. I have watched them conquer their addictions through honesty and humility, starting by going to that very first meeting and telling the truth. Even if it's false humility at first, it becomes real if you let it.

Going into spiritual life can be humbling in itself. When we say, "Teach me," the process begins. As I tell my students, "You got in the elevator, you pushed the button, and you're going for the ride." Spirituality is a very deep dying process, which means that the small self eventually must die to make way for the higher Self. How deeply painful the process will be depends on how deeply prideful you are. What's painful is not the ego dying; it is the pain of having a dying ego and trying to keep it alive.

One of the dangers of pride is thinking that you are the doer. Then you are dealing with spiritual ego, which can involve an almost shocking lack of humility. In Hinduism, the great god Shiva came to earth in the form of a monkey to show the world humility. In this aspect, he is revered as the god Hanuman. He appears in the story of the *Ramayana*, the great epic poem of India, which tells how Hanuman faithfully served the gods and rescued Sita, the soul's purity. Most of all, it shows us how to serve others with humility, and this is why Hanuman is known and loved throughout South Asia.

If you are serving the poor, teaching yoga or meditation, working with people as any kind of therapist, or if you are preaching in a church or temple, you must have humility. You must be very aware because otherwise you may think it is about you. You could catch yourself thinking, I bless you, I heal you, or I can lead you. When you think like that, it means the ego is trying to claim all your good work for itself and lock you into a place of pride. When you feel yourself getting caught in this kind of pride, remember the prayer of Hanuman, as he was starting out on his mission: "Save me, save me from the tentacles of egoism."

HUMOR

I have never seen a holy man without a twinkle in his eye.

Some say, "How can you be joyful when there is war and starvation and all the terrible stuff going on in the world?" I tell them to look at the example of the Dalai Lama. He watches his Tibetan people suffer every single day, yet he's always laughing and smiling. If you're a very prideful person, you rarely laugh. I've noticed over the years that people who don't laugh don't usually reach out to help anyone either.

Once my students asked me very seriously, "How can we train ourselves to have a sense of humor? Is there a meditation or a breath practice we can do or something?" No, what has to happen is that you notice one tiny thread; you see that something is funny and you let yourself notice it, and then you're hooked. That's all. It only has to happen once, the same as when you acknowledge love. Once you do, you can never go all the way back into dryness again.

Next you could start to laugh at yourself, because you're really funny. When we smile at ourselves, we feel warmer and lighter. Once you catch yourself in something you do over and over and over again, instead of beating yourself up and getting all depressed and worrying about your karma, try laughing at yourself: I'm doing this again! What am I? Crazy?

In any given situation, especially when your pride is kicking in, say to yourself: Let me see what's funny here. You'll usually see the funniest thing is yourself. Don't take yourself so seriously. It's the ruination of so many people on the spiritual path. Some become so serious and think they have to study the scriptures on and on and on. Really they're just trying extra hard so they won't fall asleep—and they forget to laugh.

When I was just starting to teach, I was on the phone with a famous guru, who had about a zillion followers. I think he was checking to see if I was the real deal. He asked me, "What's your interpretation of the meaning of life?"

I replied, "No, you give your interpretation and I'll give you the truth." He laughed and laughed, and I realized *that's* the meaning of life, the laughter. The sorrow that touches us all comes not necessarily for a reason, but what you do with it creates the meaning of your life. When joy comes to you, the mind says, I don't deserve this, so it won't last. But when sorrow comes to you, you're ready to open your whole body, your arms, your face, your mouth, and you're ready to accept it. When you can embrace both joy and sorrow as they come, then you have the whole meaning of life.

SHARING: THE KARMIC HEROIC MOMENT

The mystical journey is about giving back to life instead of constantly taking.

Actually, the secret of the universe is bringing joy to someone, or as my guru Neem Karoli Baba liked to say, "God is in the sharing." People are very cheap with their compliments, as though you think you have to hoard good words. It doesn't cost you anything to say, "Oh, you look really good." Whether it's somebody you know or even just someone you're next to in the elevator, you may be able to bring joy to a person who may secretly be having a terrible day, someone who may be thinking, "How ugly I am." You can come between a person and her ego. You can bring flashes of joy to another's heart.

The karmic heroic moment is when you have climbed out of yourself to do something for someone else, some act of kindness. It's the happiness we receive when we help someone, in big ways or small. It's what makes your heart leap when you see a child smile. In that moment, you don't think, Oh, I'm a hero. You think, What else can I do for this child? That's why, even when it comes to the small things, you *are* a hero, because climbing out of yourself and your pride can be harder than climbing a mountain.

While you are at it, you could compliment yourself too. It wouldn't cost you anything except a little pride. It's not pride to recognize when you do something well, it's just the truth of the moment. Pride in your accomplishments, pride in your family—this is not the pride that traps you in karma; it is just the acknowledgement of the goodness in your life, and so it embodies love in the moment.

Practices for Letting Go

These practices and others like them will help you become more aware of your pride. Once you see pride in one place, you will begin to see it in others. At first you may feel that you've opened up a whole new knot of negativity, but in reality you are just becoming aware of how the thread of pride runs through everything. If you can learn to pull on one thread, the whole knot can begin to unravel.

VISUALIZATION: PRANAM

Greet all with humility.

In the East, the prayerful gesture called *pranam* is a common greeting. With a slight bow of the head, bring the palms of your hands together, in front of the heart, touching the center of the chest, as if in prayer. In the West, this gesture feels a little odd to us, because why would we bow before another person? However, if we remember the perfection of the soul, then it makes sense. A *pranam* is often combined with the greeting *Namaste*, which means, "The God (or the light) in me bows to the God (or light) in you," or more simply, "My soul greets your soul."

To enter the free skies of humility or the space free of pride, learn to *pranam* to whatever comes to you. Do this inwardly, perhaps with the word *namaste* on your lips. You'll notice a softening within you. As you are listening to someone, *pranam*, and you may be surprised what you can hear. You can practice this with events and situations as well as people. Try it when you are stuck in traffic, and watch yourself relax. You will find yourself more and more in a state of humility and acceptance of what is.

MANTRA: THE MOTHER

Silence the voice of the lower ego.

Pride not only separates us from others, but it separates us from the universal Mother as well. To relieve the cruelty and isolation of pride, say this mantra: *Om Namah Durgaya*. The mantra consists of *Om*, the sound of the universe, then *Namah*[1], an expression of devotion, and the name of the goddess Durga or Durgaya[2], who is an aspect of the great Mother[3]. As you invoke the Mother with this mantra, it is as though you become a child, so humility naturally comes to you. Why invoke Durga? Well, do you really want to hold onto pride before the universal Mother?

Om Namah Durgaya. Say it slowly, say it fully. Say it for forty days, or just bring it to mind when you feel that pride is catching you. The more you say a mantra, the lighter and lighter you

---

1. Pronounced: "*Nah-mah*"

2. Pronounced: *Dur-GUY-ah*, with a slight emphasis on the second syllable.

3. If you wish, say this mantra to Mother Mary. "Om Namah Mary."

feel. With this mantra, you are interrupting pride so it loses its power to keep you separate. Gradually, pride melts away.

MEDITATION: LIFE AND DEATH

Quiet the mind and the soul will speak.

This is a meditation for discovering your own depth. When we meditate on death we are shown the futility of both unworthiness and arrogance, and both fall away.

Breathe deeply into the chest for a count of seven. Hold the breath and feel the quiet all around you. Breathe out for a count of five. That is the first breath.

On the second breath, breathe in for a count of seven, and as you hold the breath ask the universe to share its bounty of wisdom. In that moment, wisdom comes to you and awakens the intuition that you were born with each lifetime. You will know how long to hold the breath, until something in you tells you to breathe out. Breathe out for a count of five. So now you're listening to your inner voice and not the voice of pride.

Repeat this pattern for a eleven full cycles.

Then sit very quietly and center yourself in your chest, the spiritual heart. Mentally, bow to death and rejoice in life. Then bow to life and honor in death as well. As you watch the breath coming in and out, the two merge, life and death. You have smoothed the sharp edges, life and death, joy and sorrow, and you have twined them together in a braid. Go deeper. Love, grief, life, death, everything is changing, yet always intertwined.

When doing any breathing exercise, don't strain or do anything that might risk your health. It's okay to modify these practices by changing the number of breaths or cycles, just keep the ratio between breaths consistent. In other words, if I say "breathe in for twelve and hold it for six," you can change it to "breathe in for ten and hold it for five."

You can stay in this meditation for as long as you want. That, too, you will know by your intuitive awareness.

CHAPTER SIX

Indifference

Recognizing the Karmic Space

*If you hold back your love in one situation,
it will be held back in all.*

You go to your job, then you go home and work some more, you watch a little TV, go to bed, and do it all again the next day. Where is the joy? Your life begins to feel stale. Then, when confronted by the suffering of others, you don't feel as though you have the energy to care.

I began my spiritual life when I had a vision of Jesus Christ. In those days, I was always asking a lot of questions, and I asked, "What is the worst thing that can happen to a human being?"

"A dry heart," was the answer. This surprised me, because I had been thinking about the things that could happen in the world—wars, plagues, natural disasters, humanity's whole sad parade of pain.

A heart that is dry is one that has lost its capacity for compassion. This is what we have when we are caught in the fourth karmic cubbyhole, indifference.

Few people would admit that they lack compassion, but it is easy for indifference to creep up on us. It starts when we become indifferent toward ourselves because we are unwilling to go into the depth of who we are. Next we stop caring about others, and then our indifference extends to the whole world.

Because it can mask itself as self-protection, indifference is seductive. It's easy to believe indifference will protect our hearts from feeling the suffering of others. This is especially true for people who see terrible things every day, like doctors and nurses who went into medicine to help people but have seen too much. As they begin feeling burn-out, indifference calls to them and offers a comfortable place to rest.

HIDING FROM PAIN

Indifference dims love's light.

When you look deeply enough, indifference is about hiding from pain. In the name of protecting your feelings, the ego starts to nudge you into the space of separation, which really means separation from the living moment and the living action of the now.

To close your heart is to become indifferent. At first, we do this because we fear the pain of what we imagine others think of us, and we even fear our own reactions to those imagined thoughts. "I don't care what they think of me," we say, putting up a false front supported by false courage. This makes for a barren life, as our energies are wasted on what isn't real. Instead of vitality, we have stagnation. When one part of life becomes stale, others will follow.

Indifference to ourselves inevitably leads to indifference toward others, which can cause us to hurt those around us. I have seen people hurt others terribly in the name of their own happiness, but in the end they are still not happy. When we don't care how our actions affect others, karma catches us and boxes us into spaces that are too small to hold the glowing heart of love.

As indifference hardens within us and we turn away from others, we also become indifferent to the world. We turn on the TV and we see "Earthquake: Thousands Dead!" And we change the channel. Oh, not right away. We send money, or we say a prayer, but whatever we can do just seems small in the face of so much suffering. Instant world-wide communication has the potential to make us more compassionate, but most of the time it just makes us more indifferent. In the past when we heard terrible news we had time to absorb it and respond, but now, we just feel overwhelmed.

Karmic Connections

On the one side we have inaction, which is the reluctance to choose, to act, to do. On the other side, we have self-righteousness. The righteous person is terribly sure of his own opinions and actions, no matter who gets hurt. Neither has found the middle way, and neither can find the way out of the space of indifference.

INACTION

Not choosing is a choice.

Our world is full of all kinds of pain: war, hunger, sickness, the destruction of the earth herself. Some people feel that their own small world or even their own inner life is all they need, but silence kills, and indifference kills even more. We tell ourselves that everything is going to be okay. Well, it's not all okay now, and it's not going to be okay unless we make it so.

With so many problems in the world, there are many, many opportunities to take action. Yet many people, when they are asked to get involved in changing things, say, "Oh that's just politics. I stay out of that." So they keep their hands clean, they sit by and watch what's going on in the world, and they allow a few people to get hold of power to do what they want. After that happens, they say, "See, I told you politics was dirty. I'm just going to meditate." However, karma is the law of action, and you can't escape karma by doing nothing. Inaction is karmic too, especially if you don't do something you are capable of in the moment.

If you live in this world, your hands are not 100% clean, I don't care who you are. You are not living in a cave in the

Himalayas, and even if you were, I would tell you the same thing: Keep your hands together in prayer for part of each day, and then open your hands wide and use them to touch, to serve, to build, to heal.

"But," you say, "we can't all jump on a plane and go every place there's a natural disaster, and if we did most of us would just be in the way." That's true, but notice I said, "Do something you're capable of in the moment." Surely someone is in need in your own neighborhood, if you took the trouble to notice. Is there someone in your family or at work who is in trouble? You may think you don't have much to offer, but it means a lot to others just to know someone cares enough to reach out.

Pain is pain, and no matter what pain anyone is in, it belongs to all of us. It doesn't work to have compassion for some and not others. It does no one any good to judge or measure pain. I was told by my guru, Neem Karoli Baba, "Feed All," not "Feed Some."

Can the rich be in pain as much as the poor? Absolutely. So compassion extends to everyone you meet, not just the ones you choose. You can't help everyone, but don't try so hard to decide who deserves your help. Any judgment takes you out of love. Some situations will present themselves to you, and that's when you must take action.

A STUDENT'S STORY:
HUNDREDS LIKE THIS

Over the years we've helped a farm cooperative in rural Uganda that was founded mostly by AIDS widows. They had pooled their small plots of land to farm more effectively. Then they added vocational training programs and small businesses, and now, after years of struggle, they have barely turned the corner to sustainability. *(continues)*

I was taking a walk to look at the village's new charcoal-fueled bakery, when I found a young woman and her baby on the path before me. The mother was shockingly malnourished and her baby was tiny and listless. Her little head was dangling to the side and her eyes were staring wide open. Clearly the mother was too close to starvation to nurse her. I greeted the mother and shook her hand in the polite Ugandan way, as if this was a normal situation.

When I asked around, it turned out the mother had left the village to marry, but her husband hadn't provided food. When he came home in the evening, he would beat her. She had wounds on her head, and her leg had been knocked out of place from the abuse. Somehow, she had limped back home, but there was no family left here to help her.

We quickly found her some food. Yet my friends in the community informed me, "There are so many like her. There are hundreds. We see this every day." I knew this was true. I certainly knew that we can't save everyone. Yet I was hearing Ma's words in my head: "There are no throw away people." So, although I hadn't gone looking for her, here she was, and I could not turn my back.

We bought her a 50-pound bag of posho (a staple food of the region), clothes for the baby, and formula. Her opportunistic infections were treated with antibiotics while we waited for her HIV test to come back. The community found a safe place for her to stay.

I was amazed yet again at how simple it is to help someone, how little cost and effort it really took to save her life. After eleven trips to Africa, I still don't know a better program than this: Start by taking care of what's right in front of you.

Today this woman is doing well. Sadly, her abusive husband found her and took the baby away—as is his right in that culture.

RIGHTEOUSNESS

Never throw anyone out of your heart.

Self-righteousness and intolerance exist in every religion, as well as in politics, academics, any place where people are terribly sure they have the answers, and any place they are willing to hurt another living being for the sake of an idea. When you feel self-righteous—and we all do sometimes—ask yourself: For these principles that I hold so dear, how deeply am I willing to hurt someone? How deeply am I willing to hurt myself? Your answers are measurements of your own level of self-righteousness.

In a later chapter, I will explain the karmic space of "the desire to be right," which is another kind of righteousness. In that space, you are always pushing what you believe onto others. However, the desire to be right includes a tiny bit of doubt, or else you wouldn't push so hard. You need to win the argument, or you need to get confirmation of your rightness. Righteousness doesn't need confirmation, it doesn't just *think* it's right, it *knows* it. That's when it becomes indifference.

Tony was in the hospital in Miami, and his parents wanted to visit. He hadn't seen them in a very long time because they couldn't handle that their son was gay. In fact, they had stood on the side of the Gay Pride parade with signs: "God Hates Fags," "AIDS is Your Punishment," that kind of thing. So Tony was very excited that they wanted to visit him. He told me he was even willing to pretend to be straight for them, he was just so happy that he would see them.

When I heard this, I told him, "Just have two friends there with you."

"Oh why? They're not going to hurt me."

I said, "Just have them there; you don't even have to say they're with you." So he had his friends pretend they were visiting the guy on the other side of the curtain.

94

The parents came in, and his mother told him, "When you die, tell the hospital not to get in touch with us. We don't want to know. We do love you, but we're finished with you. We came to see you in person to make that very clear."

His friends called me, both of them crying. Of course Tony was devastated. His parents had just stuck a knife in his heart. I've seen a lot of terrible things, but I have never seen such coldness, and that's the coldness of indifference.

Karmic Graces

The way out of indifference is first to recognize it, which takes a new level of honesty with yourself. But recognition is not enough. Once you realize what has happened to your heart, you can find the compassion in yourself once again. Then you must learn to serve others. As explained below, it is possible to serve with both an open heart and detachment. Finally, the generosity of prayer will also free you from indifference.

COMPASSION

Thoughts of love bring you to a loving world.

I often speak of the wounded heart, because in truth everyone's heart is wounded. Sometimes I get tired of saying it, but every time I lead a guided meditation into the heart chakra, there it is— the pain in the hearts of so many of my students. Will our pain ever end? No, not as long as we live on earth. But, remember that the way out of all the karmic spaces is to face your pain and your fears and come out the same way you went in. To do this we must have compassion for ourselves.

Are you afraid? Are you hurting? If you are, it's a simple fact, and there is no need to hide it, cover it, disguise it, lie about it, feel guilty about it, or create a false self to avoid it. There is no need for all the ways we hide that eventually lead us into indifference. Once we can acknowledge our own pain, then we can be guided by compassion—both for ourselves and others.

Every religion has a version of the Golden Rule: "Do unto others as you would have them do unto you." When we understand the laws of karma, we realize that the line between "others" and "ourselves" is not as clear as we once thought. While we are engaged in serving others, our personal karma can't follow us.

SERVICE

Service is a form of worship.

A lot of us fall into the trap of saying, "There is so much pain in the world, what can one person do?" In all my years of teaching I've noticed that those who say, "I can't take the pain of the world," are those who do the least about it. Over and over, I tell them to get out there, do something, and find a way to serve.

Since you're always busy, you may think you are doing too much already. In reality, there's no such thing as doing too much. A lot of us think that we can't fit anything more in our hearts, not one more person to care about, not one more cause, because the heart will hurt if it stretches. I promise you, when you serve others, there's always room for one more. This is because you give your whole heart. There is always room in your heart, always.

There is great joy in service. It comes from the same place as all joy: quieting your ego-mind so your spirit can shine through. Call it God, call it the soul, call it the higher mind, call it your highest, truest Self. Through service, you will realize that you are not the doer, and that God or love is working through you. Any act of service becomes a state of surrender to something bigger than your ego. In this way the ego is put to rest. It's not taking credit, it's not confusing you with discussions of your motives, it's not worrying about its karma, and it's not telling you that you've been doing too much or too little.

Because service takes us out of indifference, it stops karmic reaction. To the extent that you have stepped out of the small self, the laws of cause and effect no longer apply to you. Do some people serve others because they think it is good for their karma? Yes, and it is true that service neutralizes negative karma, but it doesn't really work if you are just trying to buy yourself good karma. You receive the benefits of karma when you serve the poor and the sick without looking for a reward, doing it for no reason or purpose, except maybe the joy that it brings you. Even if your motives may not be so pure in the beginning, do it anyway. Eventually, it will purify your heart.

THE CHIDAKASH

Don't mistake detachment for coldness.

As you are developing empathy and serving others, you may find that your heart hurts from the pain of those you visit, the horror of their condition, the unfairness of life. You may begin to feel you just can't take it anymore, and you long for the comfort of indifference. That's why it is so important to remember: Pain adheres to pain. This means, if you hold onto your own heartache and sorrow when you visit the sick, then the pain of everyone you see will enter your heart and cling to you. This is what makes us feel overwhelmed or burned out. The person suffering doesn't need your tears, she has plenty of her own. She needs your smile, your joy, your laughter, and yes, your emptiness, even if you have to fake it a little bit.

There is a way to have both compassion and detachment, which is not to be confused with indifference. This way is called the *chidakash* and is a teaching of Shri Bhagawan Nityananda of Ganeshpuri, whom I usually call simply "Swami." He explained that there is a "heart space above the head." If you know about the chakras, you know they are energy centers in the body. All of us have the emotional heart in our chests, where we feel joy and sorrow. But this is also often "the wounded heart" because so many of us have been hurt there. We can think of the *chidakash* as another energy center, located just above the physical body.

It is a space of detachment, yet also compassion. Here we have clarity and unconditional love. By training yourself to keep your consciousness in the space of the *chidakash*, simply by focusing your breath there, you can work and serve without wounding your emotional heart. With the *chidakash*, we no longer have to fear the pain of the world or hide from it in indifference.

Sometimes, the detachment of the *chidakash* can feel cold. It feels strange not to be in your emotional drama, and that's why many people confuse detachment with indifference. Some fear detachment because they are afraid they will become indifferent. Others think they are being detached when they are really being indifferent. The difference is simple: If you are not compassionate and willing to serve, then you aren't detached, you are indifferent. The important thing is that with true detachment, you want to serve, help, and ease the suffering of someone else, but with indifference you just don't care.

Many years ago, I learned that detachment is not the same as indifference. I had gone to Guatemala with some priests to help them set up an orphanage. There had been a major earthquake just before we got there, and we were out in the streets doing what we could. I found a baby, a little girl of about two or three years old. She died in my arms.

I lost it, completely. I wanted to hold her forever, to rock her, to keep her warm. One of the priests came over to me and said, "Look over there. There are other children." There were, but I was blinded by my emotions. He actually had to slap me. "Lay this baby down and go help the living," he said, and I did. This is the difference between the emotional heart and the *chidakash*.

Although it felt cold to lay that baby down, the real coldness would have been to ignore the other children.

In the "Practices" section below there's an exercise to help you enter the *chidakash*.

PRAYER

Be generous with your prayers.

Many times, we do care and want to do more, yet we feel powerless. For example, we know we can't make someone want to give up an addiction, and no matter how we may love someone who is an addict, nothing seems to help. One answer is prayer.

There are many kinds of prayer, and sometimes we pray for something specific that we want. That's one kind of prayer, but it's not quite what I mean here. Instead, when faced with the pain of the world, practice the prayer of awareness. This means to open your heart in the presence of God in any form, in the presence of the universe, or even in the presence of your higher Self. Just ask the universe to listen to your silent wordless heart. You could do this as you watch the terrible images of war and disaster that fill the TV. You could do it as you think of the sorrow of someone close to you. You could even do it as you feel your own pain, as long as you steer clear of self-pity. Know that someone hears you, always, and share your open heart, wounds and all. In this way, whole countries can be prayed for, and the tiniest things can be prayed for; nothing is too big or too small. Such prayers are heard, although how they are answered is not for us to understand.

The breath is another type of prayer as you breathe with awareness, as you use the breath to unlock the infinite. Now the karmic cubbyhole of indifference serves no purpose whatsoever, and it begins to dissolve.

Eventually you may find that you live in a continuous state of prayer.

Practices for Letting Go

The best way to break through indifference to others is to begin to serve, and that requires you to learn detachment so you don't get burned out. When you help others, you will begin to be kinder to yourself as well as others.

BREATH: ENTERING THE CHIDAKASH

Detachment frees the soul.

You can use your breath, deliberately, to enter different states of consciousness. This breathing exercise will help you enter the *chidakash*, or what my teacher, Swami Nityananda, called "The heart space over the head."

I have taught this breath to many doctors, nurses, and others who see terrible things every day. They need detachment so they can do their work, but sometimes they just make themselves numb. They continue to go through the motions of taking care of people, but their heart isn't in it, and they begin to suffer from burnout.

The *chidakash* offers a another way to deal with pain: It enables you to be caring yet detached. You can practice it whenever your compassionate heart brings you more than you can handle, for example if someone you love is suffering.

First, breathe in and out of your emotional heart center in the middle of the chest.

Second, breathe into the heart center, and breathe out as if you had an opening at the top of your head. Let your awareness rise with the breath.

Third, breathe in and out a few inches above your head. Rest there, while you deal with pain from a space of clear love, free of emotion.

When you are finished with what you have to do, for example, when you get home from visiting someone in the hospital, return your awareness to the heart space in the center of the chest. This may release a flood of emotion; let yourself feel it, and let yourself move on. The *chidakash* has shown you the possibility of working with your emotions instead of letting them sweep you away.

ACTION: SELFLESS SERVICE

No excuses.

Just get out there, just go help someone. No matter where you live, there is a school that needs tutors, or a homeless shelter that needs a cook, or a nursing home where the patients need visitors. Or maybe you know someone who could use a little help at home, someone who is overwhelmed by taking care of a new baby or a relative with Alzheimer's. If you are terribly shy, then see if there is a project near you to build houses or clean up a park, or see if there is an animal shelter that needs volunteers.

"No excuses" is a sports slogan, and it makes a lot of sense. What's your excuse? You don't want to go out there like Lady Bountiful, you don't really feel all that compassionate, and you can't stand people who fake it. That stops a lot of people, because there is some truth in it. In fact, most people who serve have some kind of mixed motive, but at least they are doing something. If you wait around questioning your motives, nothing will ever change. Let's say you've been helping at a homeless shelter, and suddenly it's freezing cold outside, and you get a call, they need you right now to hand out blankets. You can't wait for someone to admire you, and you can't wait for your own purity to kick in, you just have to go. That's how it becomes real. All of a sudden you are in the moment.

Make some calls and volunteer. When you find your place, be consistent until you have time to get to know the people, and let them begin to count on you. (Keep a journal too. You may surprise yourself with how much you learn.)

ACTION: EMPATHY

Does the sun choose who to shine on?

Sit on a bench where people are passing by. Without being obvious, choose a person and look straight at his or her heart chakra. Do not judge her clothes or the way she walks, nothing.

Try to sense, or imagine, what the person is feeling. For example you may sense that she is filled with confidence or that she lacks confidence. You may feel happiness or grief. You may really be picking up something or not. It doesn't matter. This exercise is not about developing your psychic powers. The point is just to observe closely without judgment. Send a blessing to the person, nothing fancy, just a simple thought of goodwill. You may feel a silent expansion of your awareness. Meanwhile, you pull yourself out of yourself. You begin to understand that you contain a pure life force that reveals itself as genuine caring for everyone and everything.

Back on that park bench, imagine yourself coming toward you. Remember, no judgment. What do you feel? Is this exercise about looking at yourself, or others? Does it matter? We are all one.

CHAPTER SEVEN

Ego of Self-Thought and Self-Indulgence

Recognizing the Karmic Space

You become an exile from your own life.

Have you ever found yourself thinking about the same things all the time, feeling powerless to stop? When you are trapped in the karmic space of self-thought, thinking about yourself all the time develops deep karmic roots, because you are indulging the same thought over and over again. This cubbyhole is about the karma that arises from incorrect or obsessive thinking.

The ego is a great storyteller. It offers lies with enough truth mixed in to make them attractive. It wants you to think, think, think, whether or not these thoughts will help you. Thoughts actually take form if you let them, and reinforcing the same thought-forms again and again creates deep habit patterns of thought called *samskaras*, which follow you through life as well as from lifetime to lifetime.

When ego is in charge, it's as if you are on a stage in your own mind, just acting away! Then, like a celebrity who believes his own press, you lose perspective. You forget that there is an underlying reality. When the screen goes dark, when the comedy or tragedy is over, we are left with just ourselves. But who are we? What is real? Most of the time, we answer these questions by telling ourselves a new story, or re-running the movie we just saw. Even watching the same show over and over may seem preferable to asking the ancient and dangerous question: "Who am I?"

For example, suppose you had a fight with someone, or some other painful thing happened. You went to bed, and when you woke up you felt okay about what happened. Later, you slipped right into thinking, I'm mad about this, or I'm hurt about that. You just brought the whole thing back; in fact you went looking for it so you could bring those old thoughts into a new day. You couldn't use a new dawn to start fresh, because you were so afraid of the impermanence of happiness.

Everybody has a childhood story: "I was beaten." "I was not loved." "I was rejected." "I was hungry." The key to all these stories, even, "I was happy," is the same: "I was, I was, I was!" Now the past takes up space in life, space that could be available to the joy of the moment.

You may also obsess about how you have to right the wrongs done to you or how you have to correct all the mistakes you have made. The ego will trouble you with restless waking dreams, yet you cannot change the past. Ego catches you by always telling you to do the impossible. If you have hurt someone, an honest apology can free both you and the person you hurt, but only if you truly let the past go.

The ego may also trap our minds by calling us into thoughts of the future. We anticipate problems and dangers, and we react to pain that may never come. Karma is a cycle of action and reaction, but now we are reacting to something we merely imagined. We allow our minds to go over and over our imaginary future pain until we make it real. Yet with all that worry about the future, if something good happens, we often don't trust it.

Getting caught in self-thought has us constantly overreacting to situations because we think everything is about us. Once we overreact, emotion leads to self-indulgence. The more we buy into the reality we have created, the more we are caught in the second half of this karmic space, the ego of self-indulgence. In that space we are involved in the karmic cycles of self-pity, constant complaining, blaming others, and self-justification.

All these thought patterns take you from the present moment. If you are only fifty percent in the present, then you are only living fifty percent of your life. The other fifty percent is lived in the past or future. You are, quite literally, half alive. No wonder you're tired! Ask yourself, this very second, How much of my life am I giving to the pain of the past? Or, if you often look back with nostalgia, How much am I giving to past joy? This is all your choice. All of these ego patterns get their power from your reactions to your own life. You react and overreact, all in your mind, until you forget to live.

When we are caught in the ego of self-thought, it is easy to hurt others. I learned a big lesson about this years ago when my children were young. They had been invited to a sleepover at a friend's house. They really wanted to go, but I had such a feeling of foreboding about it that I told them they couldn't. In the middle of the night, the furnace at their friend's house blew up, and everyone in the house was killed.

All these conflicting feelings went around and around within me. I couldn't get past feeling how fortunate I was that my children hadn't been there and at the same time feeling horrible about myself, because how could I be happy given what had happened? Meanwhile, I had no patience with anyone. It was the winter and everything around me was just bleak.

I was close to many of the neighborhood children, and a little girl, all excited, called to tell me, "I have a butterfly in my house. I have a butterfly and it's winter and I saw a butterfly and I have it!"

"Listen, Honey," I said, "I can't do this right now."

"But I have a butterfly, a butterfly!"

I said, "Honey, really..." and I hung up on her. Three children were dead, and she wanted to bother me about a butterfly?

After a while her mother called me. "What did you say to her? She hasn't stopped sobbing."

I realized, I had killed her butterfly by indulging in my own emotions. I called her back, "Please, tell me about the butterfly. I really want to know." She just lit up, and told me all about it.

This is so important to understand: My self-indulgence could have changed this child's life. If nobody cared about her butterfly, she could have turned away from finding excitement in little things, and she might only have found excitement in things like new houses, new cars, new everything.

If you have troubles, even if you are in agony, the whole world doesn't have to be in agony. No matter your own pain, you can still bring the beauty of love to another human being. I remember that butterfly story and I tell it often. In fact, I had a butterfly tattooed on my hand so that I would always be aware: No matter what, do not step on anybody else's butterfly.

CREATING SAMSKARAS

Do not burden your heart with thoughts of past and future.

Let's say there's a person who actually did something to hurt you. Maybe she stole your boyfriend. Months pass, and the actual incident has no more energy to it. You can't remember what was so great about that guy anyway. She already ditched him and moved on, but you remain stuck. You still think about it, and you can't stand to be around her. So where is all that angry energy going? It's going inside your gut and settling in like old shoes that are so comfortable you can't get rid of them—but you can't wear them in public either. A year passes; soon you don't much care or even remember what happened, but you still feel betrayed.

The unhappiness you feel is not about what happened. It is about your thoughts, and you have dug yourself a little deeper into the karmic space of the ego of self-thought. Such a thinking pattern becomes so strong that it burns a route through your mind as it becomes easier and easier to repeat. Because of the indulgence of going back to it over and over again, it develops deep tracks within you. You keep going on, and although the tracks have become rusty with age they can run all the way to eternity.

Before you know it, these same tracks follow you into next year and the year after, and then to your next lifetime and the one after that, and so on. Thought has become *samskara*, and *samskara* has become karma.

Karmic Connections

The feelings that arise in this karmic space are all familiar to us: guilt, shame, denial, projection, blame, self-doubt, complaining, self-pity—everything except happiness. It's all painful, and yet we go deeper and deeper into thinking about it all because mental chaos is familiar, and the situations that give rise to all those feelings are familiar too. Mental turbulence and complaining are two key connections to this karmic space.

MENTAL TURBULENCE

The ego needs chaos in order to identify itself.

The ego of self-thought and self-indulgence is about the stories we tell ourselves, complicated, conflicted stories full of emotion. The result is mental chaos. Besides the stories we tell about ourselves, we also project stories onto other people. The story can be happy or sad, bright or dark, overly optimistic or downright paranoid, but the thing to watch for is how we make other people fit into the world of our own thoughts. For example, you go out with a new man, and you decide, Oh, he doesn't like me, or He just wants to get me into bed. This is your story, and it may have nothing at all to do with what he is really thinking.

Parents also project stories onto their children: "He's a future football star," or "She's the clumsy one." Are they talking about the children or themselves? I see married couples do this all the time; they create stories about each other until the real people, and the reasons they once loved each other, are irretrievably lost.

We get so used to the mind's noise that we cannot handle quiet. This often happens when people begin to meditate. We may actually interpret any peace of mind we feel as sadness or depression. Something feels wrong about it, something is unfamiliar, so to feel better, to create the feeling that something is happening, we induce mental chatter by checking our e-mail or (and this is pretty much the same thing) checking into an old story: My mother neglected me and I still can't find love and I will probably live my whole life alone and....

This is also the karmic space where you create chaos in your mind by constantly asking "Why?" There are so many whys in your life: Why did this happen? Why me? From "why me" to "poor me" is not a long journey. It truly is futile to ask why all the time. Pain is part of life, so you might as well ask why someone else is suffering, and why *not* you?

Don't ask why about the past, just go forward. I learned this from my mother, who I count as my first spiritual teacher. She spent months fighting cancer in the charity ward of Coney Island Hospital. The night before one of her operations, I asked her, "Why you? Why do you have to suffer like this?"

"Never ask why," she replied, "because who's gonna give you an answer?" Then she pointed at the next bed. They used to call this ward "The Meat Market" because the beds were so close the patients could reach over and touch each other. She said, "Now go, make them laugh." I was eleven years old, with not too much to give, but I could dance the soft shoe and I could sing really loud, so that's what I did, day after day until she died.

Most of us can't help asking some "why" questions. But make them count and be sure to truly listen for the answers. Why do I always reject love? Why do I do something self-destructive just when I am close to happiness? These are the type of questions that actually have answers, and by using your intuition you can use questions to trace some of your karmic patterns. The problem with asking why all the time, especially in unanswerable questions like "why me?" is that repetitive thought stirs up turbulence in your mind, heart, and energy. In that turbulence, even if there is an answer you can't hear it.

COMPLAINING

The universe waits for your prayers,
but you keep sending it negative thoughts.

Self-pity and complaining can become a way of life: "Poor me" and "Why me?" and "It's just so unfair!" This is what gives you permission to live in the karmic space of ego of self-thought and self-indulgence. Self-pity is central to this space. Without an understanding of karma, you can just go on and on this way, living in the past and blaming life.

People are always saying to me, "I'm having a hard time," or "I'm in a bad situation." They're asking for help, which is fine, but what they don't realize is that by focusing on the problem, they are just reinforcing it. It would be more helpful if they asked me, "Can you help me see how to move on from here?" Asking the question in this way prevents the reinforcement of the negativity.

When you constantly complain and feel sorry for yourself, then the universe opens up a whole well of trouble in your life, like some mean uncle who says, "Well then, how about *this*! I'll give ya something to cry about!" The angrier you are, the more the universe sends you anger; the more you complain, the more you have to complain about. The universe is equipped to give all of us everything we want or need, and we're born with the ability to draw everything we need from the universe. So whatever we think and speak about just causes the universe to send us more. Universal mind knows what we need, but it might not sort out our confusion and mixed messages. We have to do that for ourselves.

If you keep complaining, you may find yourself in the "victim" role, which is one of many ways that constant complaining becomes a self-fulfilling prophecy. If you go around looking like a victim, people will tend to treat you like one. If you hunch your-self over all the time, trying to make yourself small and insignifi-cant, then how much better you will fit in all the karmic spaces!

If you keep complaining about your health, you can actually make yourself sick. This is a perfect example of how the ego of self-indulgence takes us deeper and deeper into negativity, and how thought creates real-world consequences. If we have health problems, we tend to complain to God: "My knee! My back! My liver!" I'm pretty sure God heard you the first time. So instead of complaining, ask in prayer, "May I be without pain?" A good time for this prayer is in the doctor's waiting room. Faith can work mir-acles, but I would never tell a sick person to rely on prayer alone.

When you find a way to say what you need without all that complaining, a new world opens up to you. At first you won't believe it, but when it happens more often, you start putting it all together. It actually makes a noise, like a bell going off in your head that helps you realize: Wake up! You're on the right track.

A STUDENT'S STORY:
THE PERSON INSIDE

I did not find out until I was twenty-one that my hip sockets were not formed properly at birth. That's about when I started to feel pain, but I had to wait until I was forty to have both hips replaced. A year after the surgery the pain came back, and it has been steadily increasing for twenty years.

I had a friend who had leukemia, and I asked him how he dealt with his disease. He said he found his illness had brought him closer to his inner self. I just stared at him, without under-standing. I could not even imagine how it was possible to feel closer to one's inner self when distracted by pain. The pain in my body ruled my life. *(continues)*

It has taken me years to learn that I can go inside and reside in a quiet and peaceful self, beyond anything that takes my outer attention. I remember the breakthrough moment like it was yesterday. I was weeding a flower bed. For me this kind of work can be excruciating. Suddenly I realized it did not matter. I can be in pain and still continue to do what I want to do. It was a liberating moment for me, a moment of connecting to something besides my body. I don't know how to describe that connection except to say it is something very real to me.

Learning how to make that connection hasn't taken away the pain, which is here to this day. I'm over sixty now, and walking has become difficult. But by the grace of learning to go within, I have been able to find a self that exists beyond the body and mind.

Sometimes I get tired of it all. Sometimes I still allow myself to dwell on the pain and to indulge in wishing things were different. But I don't stay with those thoughts very long. Because I have learned that I am more than my body, it is easier for me to accept the way things are and experience the quality and joy of life.

Karmic Graces

When we get caught in the Ego of Self-thought and Self-indulgence, our thinking, which revolves only around ourselves and what we think we want, becomes so entangled that it weighs us down. Caught in a web of our own making, we may not even see how obsessed we are.

Practicing how to be in the moment will give you a tool to set yourself free. And acceptance, real acceptance of where you are, will stop your obsessive thoughts.

ACCEPTANCE

What is, is.

Reality does have many levels. On one level spiritual teachers, myself included, will tell you that much of what we perceive in the world is illusion, *maya*. This is because the world reflects our perceptions back to us. Yet on another level it is *not* just a thought that you lost your job and your house was foreclosed on. It's not an illusion that your husband has cancer and your son is an alcoholic. It would be dangerous to indulge in a fantasy that everything is okay when it's not, and even more dangerous not to take the appropriate actions for the situation you're in.

But if you're like most people, you don't always do that. Instead you think about your problems—relationship trouble, money trouble, health trouble. You keep thinking about them, reacting to them. They become bigger and bigger, until they're bigger than you. (Nothing is really bigger than you, but we tend to forget that.) By reacting, you bring yourself deeper into the karmic space, yet you are no closer to solving the problems than before.

Before any of our problems can be solved, we must first accept their reality. Acceptance is an act of surrender to *what is*. Acceptance is very different from reaction. When you accept what is, it's not so much that you give anything up, but you surrender to the moment. All self-pity disappears in the act of acceptance.

Freeing ourselves from the karmic space of self-thought and self-indulgence is a process of learning the art of non-reaction. Not only must we learn not to react when something first happens, but we need to keep ourselves from reacting again and again as time goes by. You can't change the past, but you can change how you respond to all that occurs in your life, past, present, and future. This is the understanding behind the Serenity Prayer: "Grant me the serenity to accept the things I cannot change; the courage to change the things I can; and the wisdom to know the difference."

Has something truly terrible happened to you and you just can't let go of it? It's understandable that it stays with you. You can't deny it, but at the same time you can't let it rule you. When I talk with people who have been abused, for example, I encourage them to work through the experience, even though it can be a slow and painful process. Otherwise, the abuser just goes on abusing them.

Acceptance means that you seek help, and you surrender to the process of working through the hurt. Seek spiritual help, or see a therapist, or talk it through with a friend, or find a book that helps you. No matter how bad or deep the pain is, you can surrender to getting help, as long as you don't let pride or fear stop you. Eventually, you will be able to catch your thoughts, and bit by bit you will let them go. In this way, you will change your life.

THE MOMENT

The moment washes away all things, except love.

We tend to think that our problems are here and now, so we do all kinds of things to "escape" to someplace else. That's what we're doing in the karmic spaces, hiding from the moment. This is the ego's fallacy. It is in the moment that we are free.

Time and energy go to waste when we continually give way to the ego's thoughts of yesterday's problems and tomorrow's wishes. The moment slips right past us. Very rarely do people enjoy where they are in the moment. Everyone is so occupied with their thoughts that they have no room for the true heart thoughts that come from being present. We fear time, or we fear death, so we keep running and running, thinking and thinking. We let time become our enemy, and one day it will defeat us.

Yet the moment is all there is. No matter how much you know or think you know, eventually you will be overcome by time in the form of death. But be deeply in the moment and the wheel of time will be your companion, not your enemy.

If you practice being aware, you will have the power to stop the ego mind and come into the moment. Through awareness, you can stretch time and space and live a fuller life. The effort it takes to sit in meditation for even ten minutes every day, watching your breath, can take the place of hours wasted listening to the ego.

Take three deep breaths as you read these words, letting the air out slowly each time. Now, staying aware of your breath, take a look around you. There's a newness, a freshness. This is not an illusion; everything really is different. Everything has become fuller and freer. It's that simple. If you stopped to do this several times during your day, you'd end some of your obsessive thinking and save vast amounts of time that would otherwise be wasted.

Practices for Letting Go

Ego speaks to us, and ego listens to itself speak. Freedom lies in silence. All the practices described here, and most of the others in the book, help you to find silence. Silence is not just the absence of sound, it is a substance in itself. Silence is available to those of all religions and beliefs. Silence is not a religion, it is a state of consciousness. It can be cultivated through practices such as meditation, journaling, and action.

MEDITATION: MINDFULNESS

To breathe with awareness
is to understand life in the moment.

Mindfulness is an important Buddhist practice, one most clearly brought to the West by the Vietnamese monk Thich Nhat Hanh.

To be mindful means that you learn to witness what's happening in your mind so that you will be able to separate yourself from your thoughts. Being mindful can rid your life of unnecessary pain so that you can begin to know that you are whole and perfect the way you are. Sitting comfortably, try this exercise in mindfulness:

Feel your in breath coming through your nostrils, like a faint wind crossing your upper lip. Actually feel your breath. Feel your chest rise. Say to yourself, Breathing in. Feel your out breath, the contraction in your belly, the subtle breeze through your nostrils. Say to yourself, Breathing out.

Trying to stop the mind is like trying to stop a waterfall, so don't even try. Just acknowledge the thoughts and return to your breath. Breathing in. Breathing out. Just pay attention. Soon you will catch yourself thinking about something. Label the thought: "Thinking" or "Remembering" or "Feeling pain in my knees." Don't try to stop your thoughts, just notice them, and always return to the breath, Breathing in, breathing out....

JOURNAL: THOUGHT PATTERNS

Dreams are very real, until you wake up.

When caught in the space of self-thought, you may begin to think that chaos is a natural way of life. Once you have practiced mindfulness, you realize you have a choice.

Consider a difficult situation that has been too much on your mind. You have been indulging your thoughts, going deeper and deeper into your familiar pain. Make a list of all the thoughts and emotions that go around and around about this situation. Just list them, don't write a whole screenplay! For example, you can choose to focus on just your fears. Write, "I am afraid that if _____, then _____." This can be very powerful because it lets you see which fears are based in reality and which are not.

Now you will be able to grab hold of the thoughts and ask yourself some useful questions. Write them down as they come to you, for example:

- Am I allowing this thought to grow a root?

- Am I watering it, by allowing it to expand and grow?

- Do I already have a *samskara* of sadness, a pattern of being prone to sadness so that sadness comes very easily to me?

  - Am I *really* sad?

You have more strength and wisdom inside you than you could even begin to understand. Once you acknowledge the thought patterns, you will not so easily go to them again. By doing this exercise you are actually changing your destiny.

ACTION: CHANGE ONE THING

Stop falling into the traps of the ego.

One of my students used to work with people so severely disabled that they literally could do nothing but lie in bed and stare at the wall. When he asked me how to help them, I said, "Every time you go there, be sure to move a vase of flowers, change the curtains, move a picture—but always *change one thing.*"

I am reminded of this when someone asks me how to deal with obsessive thoughts. It's possible to become so trapped in your own ego's cycle of self-thought that your world shrinks down so much that you're not all that different from the disabled people he asked me about. Like them, you can't turn your head to see what's outside your window.

The difference is, you have a choice and they don't. Self-pity makes you forget your own beauty as well as the beauty of the whole world.

It's not so easy to love yourself all of a sudden, no matter how many affirmations you repeat. It's also not easy to open eyes that have been shut tight for a long time. Instead, you can choose to change just one thing—a thought, a reaction, a small habit—and go from there, one thing at a time.

CHAPTER EIGHT

Lack of Awareness

Recognizing the Karmic Space

Awareness changes karma.

Have you turned away from your own life and not even known it? Awareness is the key to all the karmic cubbyholes, but when we are caught in lack of awareness, awareness itself eludes us. If you don't have awareness, you won't even know when you're indifferent or when you're jealous. If you're not aware that you're stuck, how will you free yourself?

We are born wide open, but as we grow older we don't always grow wiser; sometimes we just grow more dense. Lack of awareness can accumulate from year to year, or lifetime to lifetime, until we may one day find ourselves old and alone, wondering where life went, because we missed so much of it.

Being trapped in the lack of awareness can close us off from the world around us, from our own minds and bodies, from other people, from joy and sorrow, and finally from the soul itself.

Awareness can protect us from creating new karma. Without awareness, we just go free-form into life, creating karma every time we open our mouths, every time we do anything. Lack of awareness keeps us from seeing that we're allowing negative thoughts and feelings to take us deeper and deeper into the karmic spaces, which only brings more negative karma. The more negative we are, the more we call to us a dark world, or a dark moment. However, when we have awareness, we can stop ourselves from any kind of karma before we say something or do something that would hurt ourselves or others. For example, if you have the awareness that you're about to speak without love, you can stop yourself, you can change your karma, you can change your destiny, and you can change your life.

CONFUSION

The heart knows the road,
and the soul is already waiting there.

If you are feeling confused and distracted, then you are experiencing your own lack of awareness. All addictive behaviors—drugs, alcohol, overeating, shopping, working too much—are born from lack of awareness and arise from not knowing your true Self. If you think you're the only one with a confused, distracted mind, you're not. All our minds are somewhat scrambled by distractions that the ego sends to keep us from knowing what we're really doing. That just comes with the territory—the territory of human life. Life gets all tangled up, but with awareness, the tangles open up little by little, and you're left with a straighter line to follow. When there is nowhere to go except ahead, then you have found your path.

We begin to think mental confusion is the normal state of our minds, and often we try to blame our distracted state on our high-pressure careers, or too much multi-tasking, or just the general state of the world. Looking a little deeper, we can find that we are actually quite comfortable in our confusion, and often we have persuaded ourselves to prefer mental chaos to the alternative, which is silence and simplicity.

Karmic Connections

The lack of awareness lies at the heart of every karmic space, so its karmic forms are many. The two that are most closely connected are the desire for comfort and the desire for oblivion. Both of these keep us deeply unaware.

COMFORT

How many moments have you let pass?

Lack of awareness is very comfortable. Sometimes we can't bear witness to any more sorrow, so we pay less and less attention to what's around us. This leaves us retreating into a small world where we think mainly about ourselves and what will make us comfortable. This is how we develop the tunnel vision that is one aspect of the lack of awareness.

Take for example when you come home from work after a hard day, and your wife starts complaining before you're even in the door. You just want to shut her out, shut her up, shut the door, but you're forgetting that her day has been hard too, and you're forgetting that you used to help each other through hard times. Instead you feel your heart just sink and die, or maybe you don't even feel it any more. You grab for a drink or the TV remote, or you fall into some other habitual routine, and awareness is forgotten for another day. Sometimes awareness breaks through, but less and less as you make a habit of seeking comfort first.

Being stuck in lack of awareness is like having a closet full of beautiful clothes, yet you keep putting on the same old thing every single day and night just because it's easy. We don't all have the same clothes in our closets, thank God, but the ones you have are yours, and they're allotted to you by karma, which is another way of saying you picked them out yourself. Everything is there for you to use, like life itself. If you don't use what's yours, that's just laziness. You just don't want to see how great you could look.

OBLIVION

You will seek awareness when your desire to awaken is greater than your desire not to.

Being too comfortable in anything can be dangerous, because next comes inertia, and finally oblivion. When people are negative all the time, even their sleep has a different quality; it becomes a gross sleep, a heaviness that is not the same as healthy and natural sleep. Even sleep can be something we do to escape from awareness.

Addiction works the same way. It starts with escape: I'm just going to forget my troubles for a little while. Then comes pride: I could quit any time I want. It goes on from there, the whole sad spiral. A great deal has been written about addiction, but the key to every successful treatment I have ever heard of is the same. It begins with awareness and open acknowledgment that you have a problem.

However, lack of awareness lets you lie to yourself very easily. I'm going to stop drinking tomorrow, you say, knowing full well that you are lying to yourself. You never think you are sliding into addiction until it's too late. Now the drug or the drink itself brings you a different awareness that at times seems much brighter than ordinary reality. Addiction is so hard to beat because it arises from lack of awareness, and then it destroys every opportunity to become aware. Now your lack of awareness begins to define your entire life.

We often hear that an addict has to hit bottom before he or she can start to recover. This is because it often takes a harsh shock to break through such deep lack of awareness. This is why, when an addict enters a program, usually the first thing he must do is to become aware of what he's doing to himself and to others. Awareness builds on itself. Little by little, it reverses the spiral of addiction. Instead of spiraling down into oblivion, we find a spiral staircase inside ourselves and the energy to climb up it.

Karmic Graces

Awareness is available if you truly want it. You can learn to look, listen, and feel much more deeply. Once you begin to develop awareness, you will have a new confidence. You won't live with certain kinds of fear anymore, such as fear that you are missing something, or fear of making foolish mistakes through ignorance. These fears melt away, replaced by intuitive knowing. Fear will come again and again, and you will take many steps back. But now you know, and you will eventually step forward again.

When we are caught in lack of awareness, curiosity can set us free. Choosing to be responsible for what awareness brings can also lead us out of this karma. And when our minds won't see, the wisdom of our bodies can be another path to awakening. As awareness expands, we can even begin to sense the subtle or more powerful energies at work in the universe, and use them to align more deeply with our higher Selves.

CURIOSITY

Curiosity kills the ego too.

You have committed yourself to meditate for twenty minutes, but you sneak a look at the clock to see if you can watch TV yet. Eight minutes left to go, and you are seriously bored! Your knees hurt, your nose itches, and you can think of a million things you'd rather be doing. The whole trouble is that we tend to listen to the ego, which tells every cell in our being that stillness is boring, and activity and negative thoughts are exciting. Boredom is quite simply the ego's way to make you think you should be doing something else besides noticing your ego's traps.

They say "curiosity killed the cat," but curiosity also kills the ego; when you are curious about something, you are usually also very aware.

Despite how comfortable you may be there is still a little nagging voice that asks about your life, "Is this all there is?" You may try to ignore it because it seems like a very dangerous question. In fact, it is dangerous if you don't want a bigger life.

"Is this all there is?" Who's asking this, the higher ego or the lower ego? If it's the lower ego, you may follow it down a false path because the ego always looks for "more" in the pleasures of instant gratification. Just think of the families destroyed when one partner gets bored and starts fooling around. Think of the lives ruined by drugs. Consider all the small hurts that accumulate because people are thoughtless.

However, there is also the higher ego, or higher mind, which propels you along on your search for truth. If it is the higher ego that asks, "Is this all there is?" you will discover that all you need to know about your soul is available, a sacred mystery of understanding waiting for your awareness. There is no need to roam about the world searching for anything. The search for awareness is an inner path, not an excuse to look around outside of you for new amusements.

By "inner path" I mean that you always have contact with your higher power. Always. There's so much to learn, it's as if the universe is always tapping you on the shoulder: "Hey, here I am. Use me." If you habitually ignore it, awareness doesn't go away, it just says "OK, there's always another lifetime."

It's not just boredom that keeps you from being aware. There is also fear: fear in meditation, fear of going deeper, fear of change, fear of losing yourself, fear of awareness itself. Curiosity can overcome your fear. You'll still have fear, but now you can be excited as you begin to say, What if? What if I sat a little longer? What if I breathed a little deeper? What new awareness might open up if I were nicer to people? Now you're being pulled along by curiosity, and fear can't hold you.

After I started having visions of Jesus Christ, I searched for him everywhere, including a Jesuit retreat house on Staten Island. I felt myself drawn to the belfry tower there, and I began to feel that I might see him again if I climbed to the top.

I began my climb up the narrow staircase, saying a prayer: "Christ, be there, please. Christ, be there." That's all I wanted, to feel his presence again. At the same time, I was terribly afraid. On about the fourth step, I prayed, "Christ, don't be there." That's how I climbed the rest of the tower: "Christ, be there, Christ, don't be there," on every other step.

Now I watch my students doing something similar. They begin on the spiritual path with a great desire for God. Then it all gets too real, and some of them quit completely. Many others keep going, but with a lot of stops and side trips. It's as if they go three steps forward and two steps back. "Take me God … but not quite yet."

That day in Staten Island, I didn't stop or turn back. It was curiosity that carried me up those stairs and curiosity that overcame my fear as my life was being transformed.

RESPONSIBILITY

It's a big step to seek awareness. It's a step backwards not to.

You actually have to make a choice to be aware, and that can be scary. If you begin to see your true Self just a little bit more, a whole new world opens up, but it feels like there's a crater opening underneath your feet, and you have to take a big jump. You can't just stand still because you'll fall in. You have to move from where you've been, perhaps for lifetimes. This takes courage.

Can you just stay still and not choose? That's a choice in itself, a choice made of pure ego. We say, "Ignorance is bliss." No, ignorance is just ignorance. However, ignorance is not quite the same as innocence. If you truly don't know the consequences of your actions, if you're a child, or if you hurt someone by mistake, the karmic consequences of innocent actions are much less than if you knowingly do something to cause pain.

Awareness brings responsibility, whether you want it or not. My teacher, Swami Nityananda, kept very silent for months, and I would beg him: "Speak to me!" I tried everything, including calling him fat, because that would have gotten a big reaction if anyone said that to me. He answered me with stern silence. Finally he said the words that changed my life: "If this one speaks to you,

you must heed his words." (He always spoke like that, never saying "I.") By the time he did speak, my deep yearning had already made a choice, and I was ready to listen.

Once you know, you have to act, and that can mean many things, from starting to eat right to noticing a child who needs your help to changing how you earn a living. What if the next step brings obligation? What if you have to fulfill your abilities? What if you have to give up old friends like anger, pride, and addiction?

Many years ago I would help out at a soup kitchen in New York. There was a little girl, maybe eight years old, who would always come and fill up containers to take the food back to her family, but she never sat down and ate for herself. A priest who worked there pointed this out to me.

So the next time I said, "Honey, while we fix up the family plate, why don't you sit and eat?" She said, "I can't." It turned out that her mother had told her to bring everything home, as if anything she ate herself would be subtracted from what we gave the family. Now that I was paying attention, I could see she was terribly thin and she had some kind of skin condition. I told her, "You tell Mommy I won't give any food for the family unless you sit down and eat."

Then I watched this child begin to eat with such zest. She had been starving, literally, but it hadn't been in my awareness. I had figured I was doing a good deed just by working there at the soup kitchen, and I could have left it at that. It is possible to serve with a dry heart, just going through the motions. She had been getting food, but not love. Love takes awareness.

For me it was a life-changing experience. I learned that you have to keep awareness going. It's not just "fix it and forget it," you have to follow through. When you act on your awareness, your life actually becomes more exciting. You would be surprised how many things you can change in a person's life, especially your own, just simply by being aware.

A STUDENT'S STORY:
RIDE IT OUT

Most of my life, whenever I was told I was "wrong" in some way, I would fall into a place of extreme anxiety—the kind that so consumes you that you are unable to think. You only feel like you're drowning in an unworthiness that will never end.

One day, just as I was leaving work for a business trip, my boss made some nasty comment that sent me to that old place. For whatever reason, a thought came to me, wondering how long this "unworthiness" experience would last until I felt like myself again. I looked at my watch. The time was 1:00 p.m.

The feeling stayed with me during the long drive to the airport, the whole time on the plane, a change in Detroit, another plane ride, and right through baggage claim. To put it another way, it followed me for 2000 miles. As I was checking into a hotel that night, I realized that the feeling had passed sometime in the prior 30 minutes. I looked at my watch to find nine hours had passed. I thought, "Nine hours? That's not so bad. I can handle anything for nine hours."

The next time I became overwhelmed by this feeling, I had enough awareness to look at my watch at the beginning and end. This time, "riding it out" only lasted seven hours. The next time it was five, then four, and after a few months of consciously using this practice, I found I was done with this feeling in just a few minutes, and it was never as intense as it had been.

My biggest surprise is just how easy the process really was. Once I conquered it the first time, my patience to "ride it out" kept increasing until it was no longer a big issue for me.

THE WISDOM OF THE BODY

The soul's knowing often comes to us as a physical feeling.

"How do you feel?" I find myself asking that question more and more. "How do you feel in your body?" I'm not asking about pleasure or pain. I ask this question to develop your subtle awareness of how you fit into your physical self.

Maybe you yelled at your kids, or maybe you did something to hurt someone, or maybe you just sat around the house in your pajamas all day. It could be anything, but you just don't feel right. It's not even that you did something wrong, but you did something not quite right for you or someone else. As my students will tell you, I am quite partial to cheesecake. There is the pleasure of eating it, but then there is the heaviness that comes after. So when I ask, "How do you feel?" the question is meant to build your intuition because to answer it you have to notice, on a deeper level than before, how your actions affect every part of your being.

People ask me for advice all the time, and I don't like giving it. If they ask something like, "Should I marry Frankie?" I might tell them to visualize life with him and see how they feel—body, mind, and soul. "Should I change jobs?" Again, "How do you feel?" This is a habit you can develop, a way to activate your intuition, but it is most effective if you allow your body to provide a big part of the answer.

Your body just tends to be more honest than your mind, which is so easily confused by your ego. Is there pain in your belly, tightness in your heart, or tension in your throat? Most of us have so many different kinds of blocks that it's not easy to sort them out. But the answers can come to you if you let them. Sit quietly, breathe, and put your question to the universe. And wait. This is a form of prayer, and answers come in their own time and their own way. We have only to listen for them, and as we develop awareness the answers are clearer and clearer.

It might help to remember the original definition of *yoga*, a word that derives from the Sanskrit word for "yoke." Yoga is about joining and integrating the mind, body and spirit, although some of today's athletic yoga practices focus mainly on the body. In any form of yoga you practice, make sure you do it with awareness.

Without awareness, a movement is just a movement.

With awareness, it is everything.

Without awareness, a breath is just air.

With awareness, it is prana, the life force of the universe.

UNIVERSAL ENERGY

Understanding shakti is the first step to understanding life.

How are you using the energy that flows to you from the universe? Following Hindu tradition, I call this energy *shakti*, the female energy of the universe. She flows in all of us, whether we are male or female. As you become more and more aware, you begin to realize that everything is energy, everything is flowing. Yes, the force of the universe lives in you, and you can become aware of it. The universal law is love. So when I ask, "How do you feel?" I am asking, "How much love can you hold?" This is the awareness of the higher mind, or the simple knowing of the yogi and the mystic, who realize they had awareness before they had form, and they will have awareness after death.

You have heard stories of near-death experiences, in which someone sees a great light and moves toward it. That light does exist, always, not just in death. In the knowing, in the greater awareness, you grow toward that great light. You get used to it in life, and you will know how to follow it in death.

You want awareness, you want it deeper than anything you can imagine because awareness is liberation. If you were fully aware, you'd be liberated. In the Eastern traditions, full awareness equals liberation, moksha, nirvana, satori, samadhi. In the Western traditions, full awareness equals the Kingdom of God or Christ-consciousness. I can't really put it more simply than that, except to say that if I had to find another name for God, it would be "awareness." God is awareness itself. If you learned to have great awareness of your own being, you would have awareness of God. Liberation is awareness of the great awareness.

As awareness increases, you may discover that you seek liberation not just for yourself, but for the benefit of "all sentient beings," as the Buddhists say. Even if you're a beginner on the path, the basic truth still applies: If you raise the consciousness of yourself just slightly, you will raise the consciousness of the whole planet. That's why the greatest awareness carries with it the greatest responsibility.

Practices for Letting Go

Awareness comes in moments, so be ready. Be willing to see, to hear and to know. You have mind and ego to distract you, but you also have this body and you have this breath. What a wonderful place to start! No matter what has happened in the past, you can start over, every second of the day, with a clean canvas and new colors. It all starts with becoming aware of the breath.

BREATH: FIGHTING ADDICTIONS

Every heart heals in its own time.

This is a simple breath that can help as you battle any kind of addiction. Begin with a triple in breath, through the nose. In other words, sniff in sharply three times, without breathing out.

Hold the breath and place your focus on the belly for as long as comfortable. Don't strain.

Breathe out strongly but slowly, using your stomach muscles to push out every bit of breath. Imagine that your belly button is trying to touch your spine. In this way, you are pushing out any staleness you might have inside.

Do this cycle twice more, then return your focus to your spiritual heart before you go on with your day. Don't overdo it with this breath. It seems simple, but three cycles is all you should do at one time. Be patient. It takes time to develop most addictions, and it takes time to overcome them.

ACTION: WALKING MEDITATION
Stretch your world.

A walking meditation in the outdoors can bring the awareness of nature and Mother Earth into your being, and you may even forget your problems.

Begin your walk, saying, "Breathing in," as you step forward with the left foot, "breathing out" as you step forward with the right, or vice-versa. You will have to walk slowly and notice every breath. When your breath has steadied to match your steps, and your mind has quieted down, look around you. Notice one thing, like clouds in the sky. Begin to breathe in the clouds as you walk and think: Breathing in clouds … breathing out clouds….

Keep going like this as long as you want, and then just enjoy your walk. When your mind wanders, go back to the breathing, or begin to repeat like a mantra, "walking through the woods," or "walking on the beach," whatever fits your awareness.

MANTRA: IN THE MOMENT
The mind can be left unattended,
like a garden left unweeded.

In India, the deities Kali and Kala are the mother and father of time, but they also show you how to see in the darkness. Since lack of awareness is a kind of darkness, their names form a mantra that can help you get out of this space. Say, *Om Namah Kali*, and then, *Om Namah Kala*. *Om* is the sound of the universe, and Namah is a salutation or expression of devotion. *Om Namah Kali; Om Namah Kala*.

To say this mantra, your mind has to be right there, right in the moment of time. Did you just say Kali? Or did you just say Kala? Yet as you practice, you find yourself paying more and more attention to places, people and things that normally you wouldn't notice. So you bring more awareness to life.

Then after a while you won't even go into the karmic space of unawareness. The mantra will start saying itself to you. At key moments, your ears will perk up, your heart will perk up, and you'll find yourself saying, I'm not stepping into that again—and you won't.

CHAPTER NINE

Intent

Recognizing The Karmic Space

Intent is the karmic space of lost dreams.

Our intentions are powerful, especially as we begin to realize how much we create our own destiny. Positive thinking, the law of attraction, affirmations, visualization, and even prayer all use the power of intention. So how does intent get into the list of karmic spaces? The answer is in the old saying, "The road to hell is paved with good intentions." Hell is not a literal place, but it represents the experience of being trapped in the karmic space of intent.

We know we can use positive intent to visualize happiness and bring it toward us. However, intent becomes a karmic space when the ego gets between the thought and the action.

Over time, unfulfilled intentions build up, getting heavier and heavier until they block movement, creativity, and joy. You may feel that something's wrong, or something's missing, but you don't know what. Your life just feels stale. You have lost the ability to live in the moment.

BROKEN PROMISES

Be in the moment, and the moment will show you what to do.

When you make plans, you are making promises to yourself. At first, your intentions can make you feel powerful, as you imagine your dreams coming true: I'm going to start a business, finish my thesis, get out of debt, build a house.... When you first have the intention, you have every expectation of success, which is why making plans can feel so good.

However, you don't always keep these promises. For example, as soon as you decide to clean your house, your ego immediately sends you thoughts: "Do it later. Do it tomorrow. You're too tired. Besides, you don't have enough trash bags."

Or, you decide, Tomorrow, I will start my diet. It's probably Sunday, because we usually start our diets on a Monday. By Tuesday, your intentions have flown out the window, and it will be another week before you try again. During that whole week you're left behind in your cubbyhole of intent. After you disappoint yourself a few times, or a hundred times, you may think, Dieting is too hard, and diets don't work anyway. I'm just going to learn to accept myself as I am.

True self-acceptance is wonderful, but behind this thought is often a promise that has been broken again and again. What looks like self-acceptance may just be another broken promise or another self-deception. Realizing how often you have lied to yourself in the past, you lose faith in your ability to do anything positive. Now you are not only stuck in the karmic space of intent, but you have lost hope. You may as well comfort yourself with a snack, all the while hating yourself for it.

The pattern is the same, whether you've made yourself a big promise or a small one. The karmic burden grows from this self-reinforcing cycle of broken promises.

Karmic Connections

Connecting karmas are like steps into the karmic spaces. For intent, the first step can be simple inaction. Next comes procrastination. The third step begins when the weight of non-accomplishment settles around you and you can't move. Either literally or metaphorically, you're in bed with the covers over your head. That's intentional depression.

INACTION

Take responsibility for your own happiness.

The Sanskrit word *karma* means action, yet some live with as little action as possible. They avoid committing themselves to anything. Some fear the responsibility that comes from living up to their ability. They may start many things but never finish any of them. Although they may make big creative plans, they stay frozen.

Others intuitively realize that each action has consequences far beyond their control. They make the mistake of thinking that inaction is the reverse of karmic action. Rather than drive blind, they just pull off the highway, which would make sense except that the highway is life.

They don't realize that trying to do nothing is karmic in itself. Or course, it's impossible to do nothing, even if all you are doing is breathing.

Each one of us has gifts, and we can feel them running through us. If you don't use them, you may keep thinking about them, but in the negative form of "I should have, could have, would have...." The ego jumps right into the conflict between the desire to act and the desire to rest, and disrupts the natural flow between the two states. Then along come regret, self-doubt, unworthiness, and all the rest. Now you begin to think mostly about your failures, so you fail again and again, as if to prove to yourself that you are really quite worthless. All the karmic spaces link to each other, so you may enter the karmic space of pride, where you just can't afford to fail, or the karmic space of jealousy, where you constantly look at others instead of living your own life. When you don't use your gift for a very long time, it withers.

What if you know exactly what to do, and still you don't? The result is sadness, the sadness of not being who you're supposed to be, the great sadness of being an "almost." You are almost happy, almost successful, almost free. I can think of few pains worse than being an "almost," and yet this is a very common state.

PROCRASTINATION

Karma is the glue that sticks to your feet
as you try to walk away from negative thoughts.

How many of you wait for the last minute to get things done? This is procrastination in its barest form. Each person has a unique way to procrastinate, but it always wastes time.

For example, you've made your plans, and now you have to decide what to do first, so you fumble around in your mind until you look at the clock and it's already too late to begin today. Then the next day you put it off with the excuse that you're too tired, although what has really happened is that you left just enough space for self-doubt to creep in and make you tired. As the days pass, your big plans begin to weigh you down. You begin to feel dread when you look at the day ahead of you, because you know it will be another day of not doing what you promised yourself.

Now you really are tired in mind and body because, not only are you carrying extra burdens, but also you have stopped the flow of vital energy. Intent without action brings stress, and stress brings exhaustion, and like all karmic patterns these circle around and reinforce one another.

It's just natural that everyone will fail sometimes, but when you compound failure with unworthiness, the fear of failure becomes another thread that binds you in the karmic space of intent. For some, fear of success brings procrastination, because success may bring new challenges and responsibilities that they may not be able to live up to. Procrastination can also come from self-indulgence or a feeling of entitlement. I deserve a break, you say, even if you haven't done anything yet to need a break *from*.

Soon what you wanted to do is just a thought you had once, but you have no plans to do it now. Some day.... But tomorrow continuously becomes today and today constantly becomes yesterday. You miss what can be in the moment and the moment slips by you, and you do not even begin to understand what you missed. Life is slipping away. First it is minutes, then it is hours, then it is days, and then it is years and even lifetimes.

Once the pattern is set, the guilt of what you did not do yesterday blocks your way out of the karmic space. You spend more time planning than in actually doing, or you waste your time making excuses, and meanwhile you feel overwhelmed. Now, when happiness comes, you may miss it. You don't have time to be happy; you're too busy trying to catch up.

INTENTIONAL DEPRESSION

Depression is a flight from what is.

That closet is still a mess, you're off your diet again, and you have quit exercising. Now procrastination pushes you all the way into depression. You've tried to give up the habit of negative thoughts, but new negativity keeps pushing its way into your mind and body. You are surrounded with destructive thoughts that keep making predictions about things that can go wrong in the future, thus taking you out of the moment. Or you live in a past full of regrets. The situation seems hopeless. Why even try? You feel helpless to do anything different, so you fall into depression. Depression at least feels familiar.

Instead of having gratitude for each new moment, you're living on stale promises. Every dream of future happiness begins to feel like a lie, because you have lost faith in yourself. The pain in your heart now feels so right, so familiar, you just keep walking the same dark path year after year, lifetime after lifetime, making the same mistakes over and over.

Depression takes many forms, but this particular kind of depression is what I call "intentional depression," because you called it to you by always stopping at intent, never at action.

Depression is not just a psychological state; it's also physical. We take energy into the body in the form of food, and unused calories become fat. We also have access to universal energy, or shakti, which always flows through us whether we are aware of it or not. Intention without action turns stale shakti into heaviness, just like putting on an extra hundred pounds.

Karmic Graces

Getting stuck in the darkness of the karmic spaces teaches us what could be. We can use the power of positive intent to get our lives in order, to intentionally practice joy, and eventually to find the deep happiness of knowing ourselves.

POSITIVE INTENT

Reach for a higher thought.

The simple practice of hesitation helps you stop reacting blindly to everything that happens, but there is also pre-action, a positive hesitation where you make room for your soul's choice. When you are getting ready to do something, use that split second of hesitation to ask yourself, What is my intention? In this way you are asking to be in tune with your higher self. You get yourself out of the chaos of useless or uncreative activity. You finally stop spinning your wheels!

A very simple prayer at the start of every new day or every new project brings you great power, because you are tuning yourself to the flow of the universe. You can accomplish the same thing if you make it a habit to take five deep slow breaths before you start your day.

As you practice positive intent, you will feel yourself gathering your tools—the actual tools to get the job done, or the inner tools for the journey. Now, instead of drifting from thing to thing, you will know, I am intentionally here at the starting line; I am ready. Positive intent gives you a head start, one that will last you throughout eternity. You can actually train yourself to replace a negative thought with a positive one. Did you ever really listen to that negative voice in your head? If you did, you may have discovered that it is not really your voice!

You are not your thoughts, and you are not your ego.

Deliberate thought is not the same as ego thought.

The universe is all made of energy, and a deliberate thought has power because it's in tune with the vibration of the universe. Deliberate thought and deliberate movement go together, which is one reason why yoga, tai chi, dance, ritual, and conscious movement of any kind can bring us into the moment. We've seen how stagnation reinforces itself, but movement also reinforces itself as you develop a practice of deliberate movement.

You may be thinking that sounds too simple, and indeed it is simplicity itself. And yet, sometimes you really can't fulfill your intentions. Circumstances get in the way, and it would be foolish to blame yourself. Even so, you can choose how you react when things don't go your way. I remember a performer who was asked to give a concert at a big interfaith conference. He was really looking forward to it, but the conference got the date wrong, and nobody showed up. There were maybe twenty-five people there, in a great big space. He could have just cancelled, but he came out and sang as if the auditorium was full. Watching him, I understood an important lesson about intent: If you do your best, you can keep moving forward, and your creativity will keep flowing. You can be living in joy, even if nobody hears your song

INTENTIONAL JOY

If you can have intentional depression, why not intentional joy?

When I went to India, I was invited to a dinner with a group of Brahmins and pandits. First I made a fuss because all the women except me had to eat in the kitchen, and after we got that straightened out a little bit, these learned men asked me, "Why did you enter into spiritual life?"

"To be happy."

Well, you could have heard a pin drop. To be *happy?* I guess nobody had ever said that to them before. Maybe they wanted me to say, "to find inner peace," but no, that's not really it. I wanted to be happy, even though I was already very happy with my life.

Life treats us all the same. It's how we react to it that determines joy or misery.

This may seem like an extreme statement, since obviously some people have easier lives than others. Yet I experienced it in my own childhood. We lived in the cellar with pipes along the ceiling and orange crates for furniture, and if it rained the floor was wet. My dad, when he wasn't gambling away the rent money, ran a hot corn stand in Coney Island near a watermelon stand, so that's what we ate all summer, corn and watermelon.

This was all I ever knew, and I was happy. Really, I thought I had it all. However, my older brothers and my sister were used to something better, having been born when my dad was still making a living in vaudeville. When they grew up, one of my brothers went to college and became a successful engineer, but my sister suffered her whole life, going through one mental breakdown after another, and was very rarely happy.

Psychologists argue about "nature vs. nurture," whether we are shaped by our inner selves or by our environment. This is a question that can never be answered fully, like trying to figure out karma with our minds, because the answer is too complex and too individual. Instead of trying to figure it out, we can choose the path of gratitude and intentional joy, using the heart more than the mind.

Often, happiness begins when we serve, because it has to be rooted in some positive action. Sitting around just won't do it. Maybe you go to help at the food pantry because it's your regular day, but you don't really feel like it. Still you put on a smile, you give out the food, you pretend to be a little bit more cheerful than you are, and after a while you begin to feel very good.

You begin to feel more joy in your body, or you just start to feel better. Always. It's like a law of nature. Next you begin to find things in life to appreciate, to be grateful for, and you're not always looking for the negative. Boredom falls away, and depression falls away. Anything you do over and over becomes a habit, so even if you're faking it at first, intentional joy just slides over into spontaneous joy.

No matter what you have ever done before this moment, make this moment a new moment and choose to be happy. Don't think about it, *just do it*. Don't judge what you feel, just love yourself and be grateful for the moment. You can do this, in any new moment, even if you have failed before. You can cut through thoughts and actions that hurt you. You can love yourself enough to change, enough to be happy, and enough to make others happy also.

Does that sound unrealistic? Don't worry, I'm not asking you to suddenly be happy all the time, or even for a whole day. You just have to conquer a small part of each day to start a spiral out of depression.

You were made to be happy.

Happiness is your destiny.

Happiness is your birthright.

Why *not* now?

A STUDENT'S STORY:
CHOOSING TO BE HAPPY

I was depressed in high school, and one day I told my high school counselor I was thinking of committing suicide. She immediately contacted my stepmother, and the next thing I knew, I was in a city mental hospital.

The first day, they unlocked several doors and walked me into the dayroom. I was horrified. People were screaming, or banging their heads against the wall, or just sitting in catatonic states. I had just turned seventeen. Through all my fear, my mind said, "You have an opportunity to help these people." At the time, I didn't realize that this feeling would end up being my salvation.

My real mother died when I was a baby. I didn't know, however, that she also had spent time in a mental hospital. During my three-month stay I learned that my mother had actually died in this same hospital. I was overwhelmed by this news because it seemed to confirm that I, too, must be mentally ill and there was no hope for me. These were three of the worst months of my life, but that wasn't the end of it. From that point on, I was in and out of mental hospitals until I was 34 years old. I read the book *Sybil*, about the woman with multiple personalities. My name is also Sybil, so you can imagine how this fed into my mental state. I kept fighting because I was determined not to let the same thing happen to me that had happened to my mother, but often it seemed hopeless.

I was 35 when Ma began to work with many people with HIV and AIDS, and I began to feel a new sense of purpose. I never had the ability to hide my emotions, which helped me celebrate life with them, and they with me. I would hug them and

(continues)

make them laugh, or else I would just make such a huge fuss over them that they couldn't shut me out. I would caress them as they were grieving. Through their love and acceptance I learned not to be ashamed of my feelings. We would laugh and embrace one another, knowing that we shared something very special. As they died, I lived, and I knew I had to live for myself and them. Now in my darkest times I feel them pushing me to live life fully.

What I learned was to step out of myself. I realized that to be crazy or not is a choice I can make. My choice has been to know that "I am complete" and the craziness of long ago is my past. Now, the key to my happiness is service. For the last 28 years, I've managed a program that feeds people who are in need. That Sybil who everyone thought was insane (including me) is a caregiver now—most importantly of herself.

Practices for Letting Go

You began with the intention to change your life, or why would you pick up a book like this? Have you tried some of the practices from the earlier chapters? Have you looked for places where you might do some volunteer work? If the answer to these questions is no, you may be using this book to pile up more intentions and increase your burden. You may think, I read that whole book and nothing changed; nothing ever helps. I'm depressed for a reason.

Maybe you will read more books, or try one teacher after another, or maybe you will just stop trying. The world is full of good advice and good teachings, but the best advice for this moment comes from the Buddhist teacher Pema Chodron, "Start where you are...."

You are here, you are reading this book. Pick something, and do it.

BREATH: THE CIRCLE OF INFINITY

The first karmic key is your own breath.

Here is an ancient breath that can stop you from procrastinating and make your intentions come true, especially if you do it for forty days.

First, slowly count backwards from 29. Do this three times. Notice how your breathing becomes more subtle.

Now breathe in for the count of 7.

Hold the breath for the count of 7.

Breathe out for the count of 7.

Hold the breath out for the count of 7.

Do this breath sequence five times, keeping the count of 7.

When you finish, just stay still and breathe in and out of your spiritual heart for a few minutes. (The whole process should ideally take about 23 minutes.) As thoughts distract you, remember, "It's just a thought."

Remember, you can modify any breath instead of straining to do it "right."

Do you ever wonder where these numbers come from? For instance, why count back from 29? The specific numbers are based on ancient esoteric teachings, but the short answer is, any practice like this helps you control time. You're holding time in a net of your choosing. Procrastination is a clumsy and doomed effort to control time, and this breath works a whole lot better.

MANTRA: GANESH

Remove your obstacles.

The mantra to help you out of the karmic space of intent is composed of variations on the name of Ganesh, who is the most beloved of the Hindu gods because he is thought to have the power to remove the obstacles in our paths, even the ones we place there ourselves.

Om Ganapati Om, Om Ganapati Om, Om Ganapati Om, Om Ganapati Om.

Om Ganesha Om, Om Ganesha Om, Om Ganesha Om.

You say the name four times one way followed by three times the other way, which means you'll have to stay very aware, and that's the point, to build awareness. As you ride on the breath of Ganesha, you silently, slowly, and fully climb out of intent, and you begin to feel an awareness like never before.

ACTION: CLEAN SOMETHING

The longest journey really does begin
with a single step.

If you have trouble with procrastination, most likely your house is a little messy, or maybe you have accumulated junk you don't need, or you have let weeds take over your garden. Can cleaning your house be a spiritual practice? Absolutely! It all goes together, and any positive action can open up this karmic space.

Right now, choose something. Don't make a long list, because list making, like visualization, actually programs you to act, getting the body and brain ready on a cellular level. Then, if you don't act, all that energy has no place to go, and you have confused your body.

So don't fall into the trap of making long lists of things you probably won't do. Just look around, choose something small, and do it. For example, decide you will organize one closet, not clean the whole house from top to bottom. OK, you tell yourself, I can do that after lunch.

Ooops! As soon as you catch yourself thinking you'll get to it later, use this simple trick to help you get things done:

First, visualize the physical location of the task.

Next, turn your body so you face in the right direction, for example toward that closet.

Third, take one step toward it.

That's it! Unless you work hard to stop yourself, momentum will carry you forward, replacing procrastination with positive intent.

CHAPTER TEN

Worldly Desires

Recognizing the Karmic Space

When you live by the law of desire,
you cannot live by the law of love.

Some of us go through life like babies in our cribs, distracted by any bright toy that hangs above us. Others desire one thing so badly that we become obsessed and blinded to all else. Either way, we settle for something less than our true Self. Worldly desires become a karmic space when our thirst to possess some object or person keeps us from knowing who we are or what it is that we truly need.

We are bombarded with messages that tell us to desire ever more possessions, or to seek ever more pleasure. These messages come both from the small ego and from the culture we live in. However, because some spiritual paths call for renunciation, we may feel ourselves caught between enjoying the world and finding inner freedom. We may think the choice is either to focus on fulfilling our wants, or to give up everything—all or nothing. This is a false choice, because in fact there is nothing wrong with prosperity, or wealth, or pleasure, or sex. Being rich or poor, spending or not spending, is not the choice that matters. In the karmic space of worldly desires, neither greed nor self-denial satisfies the hungry heart. Wealth is no guarantee of happiness, but neither is poverty.

We get caught in the karmic space of worldly desires, not because we want what we want but because we forget who we are.

HUNGER

The ego loves the drama of discontent.

We wake up into this life with a great hunger for the infinite, but it seems so far away that we can't touch it and we start grabbing for something else. At first, we grab onto food or mother's milk, and now we're committed to the life of the body. Time passes, we grow, we learn, we explore the world. One flame of yearning has shot through everything, and it takes countless forms.

We run and we run and we run, constantly searching for something, though we may not know what we seek. We find things to fill us for a while, but the hunger is always burning in us, coming from one moment to the next, one day to the next, one life to the next, always hungry. We eat a big meal, we sleep, and we wake up hungry again. Hunger for food, hunger for sex, hunger for recognition, hunger for fame, hunger for money, hunger to be loved, hunger to possess another human being— hunger follows us everywhere as we cling to our worldly desires.

Karmic Connections

Although the ego's conscious thoughts are all about "I want," "I must have," "I will have," what the ego really wants is to take up more and more space in your awareness. If you let it take over, you begin to confuse illusion with reality, and all of a sudden you cannot tell the difference. For example, worldly desires can manifest as greed, clinging, or self-denial.

GREED

Greed is waste.

All the world's traditions have vivid images to point out the folly of greed, yet we see it all around us.

Greed takes us out of the moment. You eat something delicious, and yet even as it's in your mouth, you're already thinking about the next spoonful—to the point that you can barely enjoy what you already have. What if your whole life passes while you're always thinking about the next bite of life, without ever knowing the beauty of the now?

Instant gratification is just that—instant. Satisfaction doesn't last long before you look for more. A habit of seeking instant gratification can turn into greed when you tell yourself, That felt good, but I better get more of it. That's why greed is a slippery slope.

Because of greed, we are in conflict with ourselves and in conflict with others. When greed overtakes us, we flow into all of the other karmic spaces: jealousy over what others have, anger because we don't have it, indifference because we don't want to share, and so on.

The tightness of greed keeps us from unconditional love. Love is in sharing with others. Love is in service. When we have obsession and greed, there is nothing to give away. Our worldly desires stagnate deep inside of us, and our lives stop moving.

I never had a lot of possessions, but my dad taught me something about greed. When I was fifteen, I eloped with a gorgeous seventeen year old guy who worked down the docks in Red Hook, Brooklyn. My dad was not happy about it, to say the least. What my father wanted was for me to marry somebody with money. Since he didn't like working, this was his idea of a financial plan. After my mother died, he went around looking for a rich widow, and when he found one he married her.

Even as a married woman, I still just wanted my father to love me, and I wanted him to love my new husband. One day, my husband and I were going over to see my dad and his new wife for dinner at their apartment. First though, I went to the Five-and-Dime and bought a diamond ring for a dollar. It looked sooo good!

"Look what he gave me," I said, waving my hand around. Everybody oohed and aahhed.

Later while I was doing the dishes, I noticed the diamond was missing. It wasn't even made of glass like I thought, it was just paste, and it had melted in the hot water. I'm no fool, so I started yelling, "It went down the sink—the diamond!"

Did my father ever jump into action! The plumbers came, the pipes were opened, they started to dig in the basement. It went on and on, the screaming, the carrying on. In the middle of all this, I felt just awful. I really thought about how far I had gone just to have my own father look up to me for a lousy diamond. It reminded me about what is important. Much later I ran across this poem by Rumi, and it summed it up for me.

> You are more valuable than both heaven and earth.
> What else can I say?
> You don't know your own worth.
> Do not sell yourself at a ridiculous price
> You who are so valuable in God's eyes.

To begin to address greed, the question is, how much do you need? The answer is not the same for everyone, but greed comes when we confuse what we want with what we need. You actually do know the difference, if you take the time to listen to your heart.

A diamond ring is a want.

Living in the moment is a need.

Lust is a want.

Love is a need.

The heart knows this always, and the Self knows all the wisdom of the ages. Yet the ego tries to keep this wisdom from you.

CLINGING

Do you really want to cling to your karma?

We all know the adage "You can't take it with you." Yet we can spend an enormous amount of time trying to satisfy our worldly desires, even though we know the reality of death. Once we are gone, what was the point of having all that stuff? We sometimes saw this very clearly at the River House, a place we started near my ashram so that people would have a place to live and die in dignity.

Marsha had fought cancer heroically for about twenty-five years, one operation after another, one chemo after another. She was still vibrant and full of life, even as she went through the most horrendous treatments. When it was time to die, she wanted to come to the River House. A space was open for her, but it turned out that she had about two hundred pairs of shoes. She used to own a stylish clothing boutique, but she was a little bit too heavy for designer clothes, so for years she just collected the very finest shoes. There wasn't much closet space at the River House, so she would have to leave her shoes behind. But even though she couldn't walk, she couldn't give up her shoes. She chose to stay where she was, even though it meant a lonely death.

There was also Johnny. After the doctors told him they could do nothing more for him, he left everything behind and got on a plane to come to the River House from California. Maybe he thought he was going to a monastery or something, but the River House was full of life. There was salsa music playing, people hanging out in the kitchen, people laughing. Johnny wasn't used to being exposed to people from different walks of life; in fact, he told me he felt like he was in a Third World country, very different from the elegant life he had left behind. Johnny could give up his possessions as if they were nothing, but he still needed to let go of his attitude and open his heart to everyone, no matter who they were. After a little while, he did. He relaxed and began to enjoy his new home.

When his time came, Johnny was surrounded by friends, and I was there to guide him. At his death, he was very aware. He followed what I said to him as if he were in kindergarten listening to the teacher. He held on to nothing, and I watched his soul leave his body and rise way up. His death was simplicity itself.

I tell these stories not to make you sad, and certainly not to persuade you that you shouldn't buy lots of shoes, but they show how anything you possess, whether material possessions or mental habits, can keep you from letting go at the time of your death. No matter what you believe about death, the afterlife, or rebirth, death itself should be faced with a clear heart and empty hands.

SELF-DENIAL

You can be in the world, but not of the world.

You can get caught in self-denial just as easily as instant gratification. Both take up more and more of your energy, or shakti. Rising and falling, shakti flows through your life like an underground river. When you miss this natural cycle because the lower mind demands all your attention, you always feel that something is missing and your cravings become stronger. At this point, it doesn't much matter whether you are devoting your energy to getting what you want, or to denying that you want it.

As a woman who used to have a tendency to be overweight, I've tried every diet known to man, or woman, so I have great compassion for anyone who is stuck in the cycle of starving and feasting. Lately, science has given us some very bad news: Crash diets just stimulate the body to store more fat. I was so angry when I heard it! The grapefruit diet, the soup diet, the watermelon diet....

In India there is something known as Saint's Disease. A yogi will stay alone in his cave, high in the Himalayas, for many years, living a life of intense purity. Every twelve years there is a great spiritual festival, the *kumbh mela*, when holy men travel down to the banks of the sacred river Ganges. On the way, they pass through towns and villages, and sooner or later their eyes fall on a beautiful woman. Quite suddenly, some of them are afflicted with terrible pains, rashes, and all kinds of physical symptoms as they try to deal with lust. All those harsh years of self-denial gave them very little, like my years on cabbage soup.

Why does this happen? It's because the energy wasted on worldly desires, whether fulfilled or not, takes us in a horizontal direction, skimming along on the surface of the world but never reaching upward to a higher reality. Meanwhile, the soul never fades, it just waits patiently while you retreat further and further into the cubbyhole of worldly desire.

When I was first teaching in New York, around 1974, I tried to get my students out of their limiting ideas of what it meant to be on a spiritual path. One day, I heard that one of them had bought himself a nice new car, which was no problem because he had the money. However, he was trying to be Super Yogi, so he didn't get a radio in the car. I was so mad, I sent him right down to Crazy Eddie's to get the best sound system they had, and then I made him drive me around blasting "Earth Angel" from every window.

Why? Well, first, you don't get to God by denying his gifts, and music is one of God's greatest gifts. Second, I felt like he was trying to buy God. You can't buy God with austerities or self-denial or anything else—except love.

Karmic Graces

Neither greed nor self-denial will satisfy the heart, although we spend many years and lifetimes swinging between these extremes. Balance is hard to achieve; as anyone on a diet will tell you, it's almost impossible to eat just one cookie. The key is finding something more delicious than the world's passing joys. When we transcend our worldly desires, we experience the true depth of lives filled with generosity, spiritual yearning, and purity of purpose.

GENEROSITY

Feed all.

When my guru, Neem Karoli Baba, said, "Feed everyone," he did not mean only food. He meant that anyone who came to his ashram should be fed either with food or spirituality or both, whatever they needed, whatever they could hold, with no limits. He also said, "God comes to the hungry in the form of food," so if you really want to help people, you have to meet them where they are and give them what they actually need in the moment, with no judgment and no assumption that you know what is right for them.

Generosity and prosperity are tightly intertwined. True prosperity means you can have anything you want in life, at least if you want it enough and you're not attached to it. The universe is abundant. But, there's a catch. If you hold very tight to anything, you will find that true prosperity will elude you. If you don't open your hands to give away your time, to share your love, to offer the richness inside of yourself, how are you going to catch the moment? How are you going to catch anything, if your hands are tight like that? What if your heart is also that tight?

There's a second part of this rule, which is that you can have what you want if it doesn't hurt anyone else. This is because, if you really thought that getting what you want would hurt someone, then you wouldn't want it with your whole heart.

You can get in the way of your own prosperity if you just want something halfway because you feel guilty or unworthy. Because I talk so much about service, some of my students tell me, "I need more money so I can serve the poor." On a spiritual path, perhaps for many lifetimes, they have soaked up the idea that it is not okay for them to want for themselves. Although they are quite sincere about helping the poor, this way of thinking keeps a lot of them from true prosperity. What they want is all mixed in with guilt and self-denial, and they forget to be generous to themselves.

The deeper meaning of "feed everyone" is the sharing itself, no matter what it is you have to share. After a while you discover this is the greatest hunger of all: the hunger to give away what you have received.

A STUDENT'S STORY:
WRONG NUMBER

After almost twenty years of a successful career in business, I fell in love with a Frenchman. This led me to leave my job, sell everything, and fly to Paris to live with him. Having already been involved with spirituality, I realized I was testing my attachment to my possessions. I let go of a car, beautiful new furniture, family heirlooms, my entire music collection, and many books. After a year the relationship failed so I returned to the United States, broken-hearted, with few possessions, no job, and very little money. I returned to my career, and within three years I replaced everything I had let go of (and then some) and even purchased a home. It was clear to me it would be a challenge not to get attached to my nice things and comfortable life all over again.

Then at work one day, I got a call from a woman who said she had received my number through Catholic Charities. She had been referred to me as a potential source of assistance, and she was seeking help to buy food for a week as she had just had surgery and was out of work. At first, I told her she had called a wrong number. Still, I had just attended a meditation intensive where Neem Karoli Baba's teaching "Feed Everyone" was an important theme. So I went out to buy her a week's worth of groceries, all the while practically dancing up the aisles, my heart singing to have this opportunity to serve a

(continues)

person in need. I even got her some flowers. I felt unbelievably happy, happier than I had felt in a very long time.

The joy of service was born in my heart the day I responded to the "wrong number." It became clear to me that the greatest happiness comes from using our resources to help others—literally giving it away.

SPIRITUAL YEARNING

Yearning is the homesickness of the soul.

Spiritual yearning is so sweet that you feel your heart opening, which allows you to touch your true self. Transformation begins when your hunger for the world is replaced by a deeper yearning. As my teacher Swami Nityananda said, "You must return from where you have come." Where is that? It is that very place of creation, the only place where the hunger ceases to be. Now your choices begin to spring from your heart, not your mind.

Isn't yearning just as painful as hunger? No, actually it's ecstasy. Hunger for anything that will pass away is pain. Yearning for what is permanent and unchanging, that's bliss. Somebody once asked me about my favorite thing. Of course my mind immediately suggested chocolate cake, but in truth the most beautiful thing in my life is worship. Devotion is a risk that you take, for indeed you may not be ready to leave what is familiar to you. Yet your own spirit is pushing you toward the Oneness. The electricity in your body is also in every cell and atom of the universe. What is spirituality actually asking of you? Just to be connected to the universe. Eventually all worldly forms dissolve into the formless and you are free and out of all karmic spaces. They crumble and fall into dust. This you learn, not by books, but by devotion.

PURITY

God is not dry, so why should you be?

Sometimes religious scriptures warn the seeker about going any-where near the opposite sex, and other times they set up a lot of rules and regulations. For example, the great Indian saint Rama-krishna warned his male students to avoid "women and gold," and according to some Indian scriptures, when a yogi can look exactly the same upon a woman, a man, a tree or a piece of wood, then truly he's ready for the depth of spiritual life.

When I was in India, I got into lots of arguments over these ideas, for I am a woman, and I have nothing against gold. I will admire the form of a man, I will admire the form of a woman, and I will not hesitate to say so. Yet there are groups of men in every faith and tradition who do not even allow their eyes to look upon a woman. Why? Fear.

Yes, celibacy has a place on the spiritual path, but only for the few, and it should certainly never be a choice based on fear. There is not one thing wrong with sex, a gift that should be enjoyed, and there is nothing shameful about the second chakra. Those who enjoy sex faithfully with their partner, wife, husband, or lover have great purity. I tell them, "Light the candles, pour the wine, and be passionate."

You also hear the word *tantra* a lot, like it's some kind of sex yoga. I'm sorry to disappoint you, but the idea has been distorted and misused. True tantra is the merge of the human and divine, not the sexual union of man and woman.

I offer only one rule: Don't use sex to hurt anyone, ever. Let the power of the second chakra be softened by the power of the heart. This, of course, means that casual and exploitative sex is not okay—the quick fumble in the back of the car, the "love affair" that is about everything other than love, the destruction of families just to satisfy lust, the predatory hunt for new conquests. All this is wrong, not because sex is dirty, but because there is no heart to it.

Practices for Letting Go

Instead of practices for giving up worldly desires, this section includes two practices that can help prosperity manifest itself in your life. If you ask for what you want and trust in the abundance of the universe, you'll have no need to spend your time and energy caught up in thoughts of your worldly desires.

MANTRA: PROSPERITY

Mantras are universal and interfaith.

Attachment to worldly desires can actually get in the way of prosperity, because our focus is in the wrong place. In Hinduism, Laxmi is the goddess of prosperity, which includes the riches of health, wealth, and spirit. True prosperity, balanced with generosity, is the opposite of being stuck in the karmic space of worldly desires. In fact, Laxmi lights the way to lead you out of the darkness of the space. If you say her mantra 108 times every day, you can truly change your life, but even saying it now and then can open you up to her grace.

The mantra is, *Om Shrim Maha Laxmi Yea Swaha!*

Shrim is a "seed sound" for abundance, maha means "great," and *Laxmi Yea* is a phonetic spelling of a form of the name of the goddess. *Swaha* means something like "Hail" or "So be it." The exclamation point is there to remind you to say this mantra strongly, like an affirmation.

BREATH: THE LIGHT OF GRATITUDE

Your breath teaches you how to live in your heart.

Like Laxmi's mantra, this is a practice for creating prosperity. Sit in a comfortable spot, and when you feel settled in, visualize the brightest light you can imagine just above your head. Begin to breathe that great light in and out of the top of your head. This prepares the body to let go of your worldly desires. When you can feel the light, direct that light right down to the base of the spine.

Breathe in and out of the base of the spine five times, then come up to the second chakra and do the same. Rise to the third chakra and let the light remain there, feeling it move clockwise all around the navel.

Then ask the universe for what you want, without judging yourself for wanting it. Keep visualizing the light going around and around your solar plexus. Then let it go and bring your awareness to the fourth chakra, the heart. Now feel as if you have received from the universe whatever you asked for. Enjoy the abundance that hasn't yet manifested by simply saying, I am grateful, I am grateful, 21 times. Finally, just sit a little longer, breathing in and out your heart chakra.

CHAPTER ELEVEN

Abuse of Power

Recognizing the Karmic Space

Your love is your true power.

A buse of power is the most dangerous of all karmic patterns, because it so directly affects others. Abuse of power can be found in government, business, religion, and also on a personal level. We've all experienced it. People abuse their power every day, for example when a sales person talks you into something he knows you don't need, a parent teaches a child to hate, or a lover tries to dominate through emotional blackmail.

The abuse of power may be easy to spot in others, but we may not see it clearly in ourselves. "Who me?" we say. We fall most easily into the karmic space of the abuse of power when we are feeling powerless ourselves, or when we feel as though we don't have control. At those times, there is always someone to lord it over, such as the guy at the newsstand or even your pet.

Feeling powerless comes from a sense of unworthiness because, deep down, you may feel weak, no matter how strong you look to the world. Yet once you get a taste of power, you may grab it, and then when you have a little power over somebody else, most likely you'll abuse it. This is why there are so many problems in the workplace: A boss is in control of someone's livelihood and that gives him just enough power to develop a taste for it. On a bigger scale, the same process is involved when human rights are trampled by dictators or tyrants.

You can easily see the abuse of power within the family. Husbands and wives abuse each other, parents abuse children, and older brothers and sisters torment the younger ones. Sometimes grandparents use their financial power to get what they want, and other times the elderly and infirm are taken advantage of. The abuse can be subtle, like squashing someone's dreams, or it can turn violent. No matter the form, abuse of power within the family is a perversion of love.

THE CYCLE OF ABUSE

The reign of terror must first end in our hearts.

We take our unhappiness out into the world and give somebody else a hard time. Then the abuse of power becomes a chain of karmic reaction. Things aren't going your way, so you are emotionally abusive to your wife—just a little bit, subtly, but then she may go out and mistreat the sales clerk at the store. It goes on from there. People may become bullies as a way to defend themselves against other bullies, but there's always someone with more power, so it becomes a horrible circle that goes around and around with no place to rest. If you are caught in the karmic space of the abuse of power, it becomes an addiction, because getting power does not put an end to the desire for more or the habit of misusing it.

If you tell enough people you are powerful, they will begin to believe you. The louder you yell, or the more you push people around, the more people will get out of your way. More power flows to you because of how people see you, and it works the same way whether they really think you're important or whether they are just pretending to. It becomes hard to tell the difference between real and false power, and finally you begin to believe in your own right to control or manipulate people. Once you develop the sense of entitlement, then there's nothing to stop you from abusing power.

Abuse of power is an addiction all by itself. Yet other kinds of addiction, for instance to drugs, alcohol, gambling, even shopping, all depend on the false sense of power that lasts for just as long as it takes for the drugs to course through your blood stream, just as long as you're on a winning streak at poker, or just as long as you can keep on buying stuff. An addict is always seeking that high because it makes him feel powerful.

If you allow someone to abuse you or take advantage of you again and again, you are actually creating more karma for both of you. By assuming the victim role, you allow him or her to deepen abusive habits or *samskaras*. By not standing up to the abuser, you are hurting him even as you are hurt. You do someone no kindness when you let her walk on you.

Psychologists have identified the cycle of abuse, but what they are talking about is the cycle of karmic action and reaction. Because of the complexities of karma, it's not possible to even begin to imagine the karmic consequences when we abuse others, because they in turn may go out and abuse, and on it goes. That is why this karmic space is the most dangerous, because it always includes others. It is possible to occupy some of the other karmic spaces all by yourself; for example, you can suffer with jealousy but never act on it, so it hurts nothing but your own heart. Abuse of power always hurts others.

The Dalai Lama cautioned us in 2001, "I believe violence will only increase the cycle of violence," and he has been proven right. How do we break the cycle? It certainly seems hopeless if we consider all the karmic connections created by the abuse of power throughout history. However, whenever you see a negative karmic cycle, remind yourself that karmic cycles can go both ways, positive as well as negative. Only one thing is powerful enough to light the way out of this karmic space, and that's the human heart. The next time you find yourself abusing your power, in ways big or small, stop, hesitate, and with the greatest awareness, choose love.

A STUDENT'S STORY:
AUTHORITY FIGURE

Do you remember being twelve, thirteen, and fourteen years old? It's an age when kids start to flex into their own experiences of personal power. At that age I was bullied for just being me. I didn't feel safe at school, and I don't remember any teachers extending a hand to me. Now I teach seventh and eighth grade, and I find I'm the authority figure. The sense of powerlessness when I was a kid made me feel resentful, but now there are times when I find myself being the bully.

Sean was an exasperating, brilliant, impulsive, impish, and overly sensitive seventh grade boy whose ADHD clashed with my need to control my class. He required compassion and patience, but over and over again, when he started spinning out of control, I lost sight of his goodness.

One day, after about a million redirections, the flow of my precious lesson plan upended, my credibility with other kids ebbing in front of my eyes, Sean's defiance pushed me to the boiling point.

"Sean!" I growled. "The hallway. Now!" I felt the full force of my anger and my authority over Sean in that hallway as I walked towards him with a fire in my heart and eyes. With each step I took toward him, Sean backed up, his brown eyes peering up into my own with an intense mixture of fear and hurt. I felt my body grow tall as I literally had him backed against the wall. I started to dress him down but was stopped cold by a shudder that passed through his body. He was cowering, and there I saw myself and my own schoolhouse feelings reflected back at me in the mirror of Sean's eyes. In that one instant, I saw my anger married to my need for authority, and there I was, abusing my power over a kid. I felt profoundly humbled, and a little horrified.

(continues)

I caught my breath. What I most wanted from grown-ups when I felt my own back against the wall in school was to be understood and valued for who I was.

"Sean, I'm sorry for getting so angry," I admitted as I felt my heart rate even out. "It's just so frustrating to be interrupted over and over again. Can you understand that?"

Sean nodded, and it was then that I realized that his lack of impulse control was driving him crazy, too.

So we brainstormed some strategies on how to work together. For the rest of the year, we had tough days and imperfect efforts, but Sean and I built a relationship on a foundation of trying our best with one another. Even when our best was not very good, that commitment to trying meant something. Remembering to see Sean's goodness softened me in a truthful way, and maybe, too, helped to heal the cowering kid still inside me.

Karmic Connections

Power in itself is not bad, but it can be dangerous for both the one who has it and the one who is being subjected to it. Any use of power without heart can lead to abuse, whether on a small orlarge scale. As we have seen, the abuse of power comes in many forms.

BULLYING

Religion carries a heavy burden of false power.

As a kid running around the streets of Brooklyn, I saw that somebody was always beating on somebody else, usually on whoever was weaker. I especially saw this when I was hanging out with the homeless under the Boardwalk. We'd actually see people arrive in packs, just looking for somebody to beat up. People will do things in a crowd that they would never do alone. That mob mentality can carry over into riots, killings, even wars. Wars are fought for all kinds of reasons, but many wars come wrapped up in the name of God, and people everywhere claim to have God on their side: "I can kill, because I do it in God's name."

The simplest truth is, when you forget the human heart, you forget God.

One time visiting a hospital with a group of my students, I found a minister yelling at a young man who was near death. He was standing over his bed, literally pounding on his Bible, screaming, "You're going to hell. Repent!"

The young man, Rick, was clutching the bedrails, like a death grip. He didn't want to live, but he was too scared to die. He was just hanging there, clinging between life and death. After we got the preacher out of the room, I climbed onto the bed with Rick and held him in my arms, telling him over and over not to be afraid, that it was okay to let go, and that God loved him. One needs to be wide open at the time of death. Karma is written on the breath, and if you have fear, fear goes with you into death; it rides that last out breath. Rick calmed down a little bit, but he still died with a lot of fear.

What about the preacher? He meant well, according to what he believed. Yet, he was speaking from the power of the mind, dressed up as religious doctrine, so I have to count him among the bullies. When we put anything, including religion, ahead of love, our devotion can take us into abuse of power.

ATTRACTION TO POWER

The soul surrenders not in defeat but in oneness.

Many of us seek leaders to guide us or teachers to show the way. Sometimes we are attracted to those in positions of authority just to feel more powerful ourselves by association. People fall in love with power, and if religion or spirituality is involved, they can confuse it with devotion.

There is nothing wrong with admiring leaders or following their guidance, so long as we are aware of the dangers of such attractions. We have all heard about political leaders, teachers, gurus, and priests who abused their power—some who got rich, some who had sex with their followers, and even charismatic leaders who led their followers to suicide.

In spiritual circles, some students may even confuse being taken advantage of with some kind of spiritual surrender. How do you know whom to trust? You don't want to judge, yet people who trust too blindly seem to end up in bad situations. If you are struggling with these questions, here are four thoughts that can help:

First, if you follow the guidance of a spiritual teacher who falsely claims to have special powers, that teacher becomes responsible for your karma. You, the student, are actually home free, while the teacher is in deep trouble—a thought that can be reassuring if things begin to feel wrong.

Second, as soon as you hear "my way is the only way," it's time to move on. There are infinite paths in life; you always have choices.

Third, we all learn from everyone we encounter. If you have been learning from someone and you go beyond your teacher, what's wrong with that?

Fourth, look at the people around a leader. Do they serve? Do they laugh? Do they seem to be motivated more by fear or by love? It's easier to look at someone's followers than at the leader, whose charisma can cloud your judgment. Look with your heart, look with your intuition, and try to keep your judging mind quiet.

OCCULT POWER

A happier person makes a stronger prayer.

Some people who enter a spiritual path get distracted by occult or magical powers, or what in India are called *siddhis*. When I was first opening up to spiritual life, I read Paramahansa Yogananda's great book *Autobiography of a Yogi*, which is full of miracle stories. Yogananda tells these stories to show that *siddhis* are futile if they don't take you toward God, but it's all so interesting that we tend to forget that.

It made me wonder if I could use my power to pick a winning lottery number. How about a horse? Then I heard that if you put lettuce in a box and prayed over it every day, with enough faith, it would turn into hundred dollar bills. After a month I just had a shoe box of soggy lettuce. The power I wanted most was to be able to eat anything and not gain weight, and I never got that one either.

What makes power abusive is how we use it, not where it comes from. This is true of both inner and outer power.

POWER WITHOUT LOVE

The seven chakras are like bright bridges
between heaven and earth inside our own bodies.

When I was younger I used to wonder how the leaders of the world got to be so powerful, because it didn't seem to me that it was because they were so wise or good. We look around the world and we say, "Wait, how did *that guy* get into a position to do so much harm?" Once I became a student of spirituality, I found the answer. It lies in the movement of inner power.

The real nature of our inner power, the same power that moves the universe, is love. When we forget the love and focus on the power, trouble begins. Our inner power, which Eastern philosophies call *kundalini* or *shakti*, rises upwards from the base of the spine to the top of the head, through the seven chakras, energy centers. The lower centers keep us grounded in life, and the higher centers take our awareness to higher realities. Eastern traditions have taught about these energy centers for thousands of years.

There is a lot of power in the first and second chakras, which flow together into the third chakra located in the belly or solar plexus, the home of our personal power. Spiritual power rises and continues upward from there, into more subtle realms. The fourth chakra, or the heart space in the center of the chest, is where we feel love. As power reaches the fifth chakra, located in the throat, we discover that we can speak words of great eloquence. If we are in balance, the love in the heart chakra can join with the expressiveness of the fifth chakra to touch the world.

But often it goes wrong. For some, the heart has been wounded too many times, so now it stays closed. If the heart is not open, one of two things can happen: Either power becomes stuck in the third chakra, or it skips the heart chakra and goes to the throat.

The first way, being stuck in the third chakra of power, doesn't mean we never feel love or a higher calling, or that we aren't creative. However, it leads us to live most of the time in a world of power relationships, and we understand life only from that perspective. If life is centered in the third chakra, it just seems natural to seek power and not to worry about misusing it.

The other way is when inner power continues to rise out of the third chakra, but it takes a detour *around* the closed heart and goes directly into the throat chakra. If you take the immense power of the lower chakras and bypass the heart, you can learn to speak and project your wishes with great authority but little love. Now you can manipulate others, perhaps even rule whole countries, start wars, commit atrocities, and not care who you hurt. Once you are set in this pattern, it will be difficult for your heart to open again because to touch the heart is to feel vulnerable, and possibly to acknowledge all the harm you have done.

As we look around the world at all the powerful but uncaring people, we begin to understand abuse of power in a new way. It is actually abuse of inner power, or shakti. It is power without love, which is only weakness, not strength.

Karmic Graces

Sometimes stepping away from a karmic space requires making a powerful decision. How do you choose to live? If you choose not to cause harm to another, then that choice must live in every moment. The remedy for the abuse of power is to choose not weakness, but a powerful love, which can begin with simple kindness. Love is most powerful when it takes its strength from the feminine power of the universe, shakti.

KINDNESS

Kindness is all the armor you need
to walk this earth each day.

Ahimsa is a Sanskrit word meaning "Do no harm," and it is an important part of Eastern philosophies such as Hinduism and Buddhism. What this means is to be kind and practice nonviolence toward other living beings, including animals and the earth herself. Just choosing to act with kindness, from one moment to the next, makes it less likely that you will abuse power. I've always said that I teach spirituality, not a religion, but if I had a religion, my religion would be kindness. When we practice kindness, our negative behavior begins to disappear. Karma begins to melt in our hearts, which open wide. There is more in the world to be seen with an open heart. Power can't just go around a wide open heart, because it takes up so much space within us.

One time when I was a very little girl, I wore my bathing suit to school. I couldn't find any clean clothes, and there was nobody around at home to help me. In class, all the kids were pointing and laughing at me. That's when my teacher, Mr. Lipschitz, said, "Oh, look how smart she is. She can go straight to the beach after school. Tomorrow, let's everybody wear bathing suits, and we'll play with the water sprinklers at recess." In that one act of kindness, he became my hero, and I have never to this day forgotten him.

If you take action to put kindness in the world, you will start to forget your small self, the karmic self. As the small mind quiets, you will allow your God mind to shine through. Fear and the need for power and control will gradually leave you.

THE FEMININE

This is the time of the feminine.

The intricate workings of karma are beyond the grasp of the human mind, yet karma can be understood by the intuitive heart. We often think of intuition as a feminine power, though it is possessed equally by both men and women.

Human beings the world over have been raised from infancy to believe in power, and to seek it. This holds more true for men than women. They exert power over their wives and children, then over other men, and over the earth herself. Women certainly can abuse power too, so I am not criticizing men. The important point is that we are all gradually recognizing the feminine power within us, and that is the power of an awakened shakti.

As described in Eastern philosophies, shakti is the feminine creative power of the universe. The metaphysics of these teachings tell us that the universe is made up of masculine and feminine energy.

There is form, and there is formless, and the universe dances between the two, or perhaps we should say the universe simply *is* the dance. Form is everything you can touch, everything you can think, everything you can name. Form is the Mother. Everything else, what you cannot know, touch or experience with your human mind, is the formless, the nameless, or what we sometimes name "The Father." One is not higher than the other.

We recognize the Mother in the esoteric teachings of kundalini yoga, which describe how kundalini, or shakti, rises within us from the base of the spine to the crown of the head, seeking to merge with the formless. When this is fully achieved, we pass beyond the state of being separate from our Self into a state sometimes called "liberation," "samadhi," or "Christ consciousness." Whatever you call the ultimate awareness, it is in the merging between form and formless, Mother and Father.

The Mother is all around us, and in fact she *is* us and she *is* this universe we inhabit. All the energy in the universe is the same. When you become aware, truly there are no boundaries.

Awareness expands, until you cannot do anything that will harm yourself, or another person, or any living being. It all flows together. Each living creature is the Mother speaking to us. She manifests as Mother Earth, as the Goddess, as intuition, as every branch of art and learning, as everything we know or hope to know. She loves all her children the same, saint or sinner, without judgment. She holds us, cradles us, nourishes us, and offers to take us with her on the journey to the ultimate. Your intuition is none other than her voice, and your power is none other than the shakti of the universe.

Power alone is nothing. Shakti, however, represents the ultimate: power and love together.

Practices for Letting Go

The abuse of power is quite simply the abuse of the Mother within you. As shakti, she asks you to turn deeply into yourself, into your heart, and feel the love and wisdom that is yours. In her manifestations as goddess, she offers you her help.

BREATH: THE MOTHER'S HEART

When you plant a seed of love, it is you that blossoms.

This breath helps you merge power with love.

Sit quietly and breathe in and out, making the breath go deeper and deeper. Then breathe in and out of your heart for five full deep wonderful breaths, saying to yourself, "I am love, I am loved."

Once you feel centered in the heart, bring your awareness to the base of your spine. As you take five full deep breaths, the heart's awareness of love will touch your lower chakras, where power resides. Now move your awareness up your spine to each chakra, breathing deeply three times in and out of each one. When you reach the top of the head, breathe in and out three times, and then return to the heart chakra, where you are truly ready for the flowing of the Mother's love to touch you. Breathe in and out of your heart chakra, taking time to ground yourself in the heart. Then just let the breath become normal. Allow yourself to feel the essence of shakti, the union of power and love, more than ever before.

MEDITATION: KALI

She becomes dark as you become light.

Sometimes you just can't find your way out of a karmic trap, and if feels as though darkness threatens to overwhelm you. In Hindu iconography, the goddess Kali is the Black Mother of the night.

She is portrayed as black because she is darker than any other darkness, even your own, and as all-devouring because she is hungry to swallow your burdens, including the ones you cling to most tightly. She is sometimes depicted as a wild woman, even a madwoman, as she breaks apart the cement of old karma.

Although her portrait may be terrifying, the Black Mother will never hurt you.

Symbol or reality? Does it matter? If you ask her to, she will devour all your negativity and leave you with just purity of heart. Just make Kali a simple offering in your mind: Mother, take my pride, or my jealousy, my anger, my abuse of power.... It can be just that simple. You can seek her help in the intensity of prayer or in a moment of simple hesitation as you go through your day. Don't take this lightly, because once you invoke the Mother Kali, as with all prayers, the result may not be exactly as you imagined. Kali may frighten you, but what she offers is exactly what you seek—freedom from the limits of ego.

CHAPTER TWELVE

Desire To Be Right

Recognizing the Karmic Space

Who is right and who is wrong? Does it matter?
The moment is free.

How committed are you to always having the last word? Do you invest a lot of energy into promoting your point of view? Can you allow others to be right at least part of the time? Can you listen to others?

Why is it that if we think we're right, we have to prove it? If we're right, we're right. No one is keeping score except us. Yet, in the space of the desire to be right, every mistake we make brings self-judgment. We think that being wrong confirms our limitations and our unworthiness, so we can't allow ourselves to be human.

Pride, at times, is the mother of the desire to be right. This karmic space has the tightest borders. In it, we are closed in by our own lack of humility. We can't focus on anything other than the idea that "I am right." Next follows, "I am right and all others are wrong." What a lonely road to walk always thinking you are right! It is the loneliest road of them all.

Can you begin to understand how small your life becomes when you think that you are always right? Notice I'm not talking about *being* right. The space is called the *desire* to be right. It is this desire that causes you to not listen to anyone else, not even your own intuition. It is a kind of deafness that you bring to yourself. It is also a blindness that does not allow you to see the perimeters of life around you. You are never open to new ideas or new ways of life. You are not even open to your own heart. You are stuck year after year or lifetime after lifetime in thinking your way is the only way. Sadly, for the most part, you are not aware of being caught up in this space.

If we are forced to defend ourselves as children, we may grow into adulthood keeping that habit of defensiveness, especially if it connects to our *samskaras*, deep karmic patterns. The ego mind tells us, "You have always been on the defensive, so there must be great danger." But what is this danger? Often the danger is that we will feel shame. Shame manifests from deep unworthiness. The ego cries out that we must be right, that we have to be right or else we will feel shame—and we believe it. As the pattern circles around on itself, it may not even be shame about anything we have actually done; it is just the shame of possibly being wrong. We are now defending ourselves against our own self-judgments. The ego, with its feeling of unworthiness, just assumes there is something to be ashamed about, and it tells us that the only way we can avoid shame is to always be right.

Often, the desire to be right comes from projection, which is when you perceive your own faults in others. One aspect of this is when you think, If I criticize others, then perhaps no one will see it in me. Another way to defend your rightness is to provoke someone to respond to your criticism. Now you can immerse yourself in a great and wonderful argument, which you can use as a distraction from your own faults. This dispels loneliness because now you have someone to fight with! Sooner or later, the victims of your projections and judgments either walk away in tears or strike back in anger. You lose friends, but you do not lose any of your own darkness. This is how the insistence on being right can devastate personal relationships, driving apart friends, husbands and wives, parents and children.

What do you really want? Are you searching for God? Are you looking toward the great wonderment? Or, instead, are you ready to fall face down in the mud so that they place a flower over you as you suck up the dirt of the world, just to hear, "She was right."

In truth all they would be saying is, "She wanted to be right. And that is all she wanted. No matter what the cost."

THE LONELIEST SPACE OF ALL

You place yourself in solitary confinement.

The desire to be right builds high walls around people, walls made entirely of thought. When we become attached to being right, we begin to disconnect from others, thinking that they do not understand us. Who needs them? we say to ourselves. As children, if no one ever listened to us, we may feel that no one listens to us now. If we really *are* right, and still no one listens, we go deeper into isolation. You don't want to hear what I have to say? Fine then, I won't talk. If you follow this pattern to the end, you will be all alone. This is also how the desire to be right can stop you cold in your career; no matter how brilliant you are, people may just stop listening to you if you never listen to them.

Even when you care about someone, the desire to be right can be poisonous. Often it masquerades as a desire to "help." For example, you hear a friend express an opinion, and you think, I must tell him he has it all wrong, and it's stupid of him to think this way. You convince yourself that you're helping him by dispelling his ignorance, when, in fact, your true goal is not to help him but to show the brilliance of your own position.

If you're married or in a relationship, you may think, I want him (or her) to be happy, and if he changes he will be; I can help. But change is never easy for anyone, and no one changes for anyone else. You are both going to get hurt. Sometimes nagging replaces love. If you fall into this trap, the ego has conned you again, as the desire to be right pretends to be about helping someone.

Inevitably, the desire to be right leads to conflict. In a friendship or relationship, it starts when the person who is most committed to being right starts criticizing the other person, making him or her terribly sad; after a while, as the friendship deteriorates, both feel sad. Nobody wins. As soon as you find yourself in this situation, it's a good time to surrender to the moment by letting another person be, and love her anyway. The more space there is in a relationship, the more the relationship will flourish.

What if you actually are right, and you know it? I am not suggesting that you let people walk on you, and I don't mean that you shouldn't care about what goes on around you. I am only talking about this little cubbyhole of righteousness that bursts with the thread of anger, the space where the desire to be right costs more than it's worth. You usually lose more than you gain from the desire to be right; you lose friends, you lose time, you lose yourself. There is something pathetic about any one of us demanding to be right, because it means that there are no more goals to achieve and nothing left to learn. That box, that cubbyhole, that karmic space, becomes so small that the walls close in. This desire to be right destroys you, and you weep and die alone.

A STUDENT'S STORY:
WHO'S RIGHT?

My political party had finally nominated its presidential candidate, so it was time to grab some campaign literature and start going door to door, just as I've done in every election cycle since 1968. I read a lot, I stay up with the news, and I consider myself better informed than most people. Despite the heat in Florida in September, I was pretty sure I was doing something worthwhile going door to door, even when, once in a while, someone threatened to sic his pit bull on me. I just thanked them and moved on down the street, meanwhile thinking dark thoughts about the state of American education. *(continues)*

I stopped at a friend's house after an afternoon of this. She had started her election research that very day by Googling my candidate's name. All kinds of Internet craziness had popped up, which she was quoting to me. So I called her stupid. Actually what I said was, "Why are you reading all that stupid stuff? You'd have to be from another planet to believe that!" But she felt I had called her stupid. Then she accused me of always having to be right, and I accused her of always having to be right, and we said some pretty nasty things. We're both Ma's students, and we were not above twisting the teaching and using it as ammunition. Since there was a bit of truth in what she said about my righteousness, the only thing left for me to do was stomp out, and we didn't really talk to each other much after that, certainly not about politics.

Ma once said, "It doesn't matter if you're right—if you hurt someone then you're wrong." That's been a hard one to wrap my head around, but I've come to see that it's true. There was no reason for my friend and me to hurt each other. She voted for my candidate, which she would have done whether we had had our little fight or not, so what was the point? This doesn't mean I will stop trying to persuade people to my point of view, but it does mean I will be more careful not to step on them.

Karmic Connections

Demanding to be right is a very hard, often lonely way to live, and it adds to the power of every other karmic space. Most of the time, with this karmic space, the person you hurt the most is you. But false clarity, bigotry, and righteousness take the desire to be right to a whole new destructive level.

FALSE CLARITY

You are so crisp in your knowledge. And so certain.

At times we think we know everything, understand everything, and, for a little while, this satisfies our need to be right. Everything seems so clear that we think with relief, OK, I've got it now.

Placing too high a value on mental clarity can become an enemy of love because, if we know everything, then we may think love is not the answer. The ego mind, in its brilliant deceptive clarity, tells us that love is fuzzy, love is foggy, love is just emotion, and no one can think straight in the fog of love. But real love is not a fog. Love is clarity itself.

Once we form strong opinions about anything—including politics and religion—we tend to cut out any voices that challenge us. So we attend just one church, watch just one news channel, read only certain kinds of books or web sites because it is so very comforting to hear our own ideas confirmed. Once again we have been seduced into a space that seems comfortable, familiar, welcoming. Actually it is a trap. The desire to be right has become a form of addiction.

On a personal level, false clarity takes on many forms, such as defensiveness, fear, and even stubbornness. When we project it onto the world, it becomes righteousness, bigotry and conflict. For those who lead others, false clarity can become a heavy burden.

Many powerful people have a certain charisma that causes others to want to follow them. This comes with great responsibility, however. Such leaders can easily surround themselves with those who agree with them, or at least with those who pretend to. What if no one ever questions them? Then they are in great danger. As they lead and direct others, especially if they do so in the name of God, they can lose, little by little, whatever gift has been given to them.

BIGOTRY

Bigotry is a failure to see that all souls are equal.

Often, we just go where the familiar welcomes us. We just assume that whatever is new to us is weird. Therefore we judge the beliefs of others.

Once you accept that which is most familiar and try to press it on someone else, then everything you are, everything you ever were, becomes like cement in a hard-hearted quest to prove you're right. All other desires—for money, sex, even power—fade within the shadow of the desire to be right. I've seen people throw away their whole lives for what they call a principle, only it wasn't really a principle at all, just the proud and stubborn attachment to being right.

Bigotry is not just about religion, nor is it just about race or gender. It's all around us. When I was growing up in Brooklyn in the 1950s, I saw that a lot of people were deeply prejudiced against gay people. Now I know that the soul has no gender, and homophobia is pointless as well as cruel.

Soon after I began to teach, I married two women to each other. It wasn't official, of course, but I saw the love between them, and nothing else mattered. That was in 1975, and since then I have blessed the unions of hundreds of gay and lesbian couples. If the soul has no gender, then this means love has no gender either.

I used to have a show on cable in Los Angeles. We were putting together a program about living with AIDS, and I asked Anton to be on it. "No," he said. "If I go on TV, I won't have a mother anymore." That's how it came out that his mother didn't know he had AIDS and that she was even in deep denial that he was gay. Eventually he went home to die, and his mother took care of him. She took care of his body, anyway. I went to see him and found her holding him in her arms, looking just like the Mary of the Pietà holding her dying son. Anton was nothing but skin

179

and bones by then. She was whispering to him over and over, "Say you're not gay; say you're not gay." He couldn't say it, and he never did.

She was speaking from her desire to be right, and her terrible need for him to confirm what she wanted to believe. Nothing else mattered. She couldn't let him die in peace, and he couldn't deny his own truth to give her the false peace she wanted. They fought each other to the end.

INTOLERANCE

There is no judgment in God, just in religion.

We are all too familiar with what happens when the desire to be right mixes with the power of religion, leading human beings to do terrible things to each other. This is why, when people come to see me, I often say to them, "Teach me. Who do you worship? Show me how you worship so I can worship that way too." That makes my God and my life not small, but so much bigger.

I have simply never seen the point to religious intolerance or the idea that we are only allowed to embrace one faith. Once, when I was participating in a meeting of spiritual leaders as part of the Parliament of the World's Religions, I saw this in a real way. We were getting ready to ratify a document called *Toward a Global Ethic*, but first we were being introduced to each other.

"Will all the Christians please stand," asked the president of the conference. I stood up, of course, thinking of the Christ who had awakened me to his love.

"Who here are Hindus?" he asked. I, of course, stood again. I love all the gods and goddesses, and I follow the Hindu path of unity. My assistant, Yashoda, started tugging on my sari to make me sit down. If she didn't stop, pretty soon I would be standing there with nothing on. I sat again.

"Now will the Buddhists please stand?" I was beginning to feel like a jack-in-the-box, but how could I deny the great silent path of the Self? I got a firm grip on my sari and stood up.

"Who here is of the Jewish faith?" Well, of course, I was raised Jewish. Yashoda saw where this was going and she gave up.

I stood up for every religion as they were called out. I didn't plan this, and I wasn't trying to be funny. I love all ways. I had to honor the God inside myself and in everyone.

I would rather have a kind heart and no religion than be deeply religious with a heart that is brittle and made of the stone of right-eousness. It is the human heart that keeps all the religious traditions alive. Back then, I claimed all paths, but over the years I have learned to simply say instead, "My only religion is kindness."

No religion has an exclusive claim to love, or prayer, or goodness. Yet every path and every religion has some leaders who will say, "My way is the only way." Such words create great karmic turmoil. I remember one TV preacher, right after 9/11, announcing that Ground Zero had been desecrated because an interfaith service had been held there. I thought of those who had died there. I thought of all those who worked on the cleanup, who gave their hearts and their souls, men and women who came home ragged, tired and grief-stricken every day. It was the hearts of all these people that made it sacred ground, and no preacher could ever change that.

Karmic Graces

When you are committed to always being right, you cannot feel your own divinity. The ego keeps you closed to new ideas or new ways of life; it actually makes your life smaller. If you let go of the desire to be right, the heart can blossom like a lotus emerging from the mud, emerging from a dark space, from the shadow of life mis-understood. All of a sudden you can breathe, you can hear the sounds of the birds, see the sun beginning to rise, smell the flow-ers, all because the desire to be right no longer occupies your mind.

All those arguments that you rehearsed and replayed over and over in your mind are gone, leaving space for the moment. By being open and learning to listen, you'll find being right isn't so important after all.

OPENNESS

Why do you make your life small?

The natural flow of karmic actions solidifies when we repeat the same mistakes. To learn from our mistakes requires openness. By allowing yourself to be open, you will be able to listen to your heart. When you admit that you are not happy in this karmic space, you can allow the light of humility to show you a way out. You will become more aware of other ways of thinking and doing.

Openness combined with humility lets you admit that you may be wrong, at least once in a while. With this openness comes new power, because when you keep your heart and mind open, you raise the level of the universal energy flowing through you.

There is a Tibetan teaching: *Always consider that you are wrong.* This is a powerful practice because it means you never allow yourself to be attached to being right. Through this practice, you can gain great strength. Besides, it can save you a lot of trouble.

In the same way, give yourself the universal permission to be wrong. Where is the fight if each person in an argument is willing to admit, "Okay, I'm wrong"? Maybe you're not actually wrong about this particular thing, but someplace in your life, in your day, in your moment, you have been wrong. So go ahead and admit to being wrong in this moment, for all moments are the same anyway.

Sometimes all this effort goes into winning an argument that is based on a simple misunderstanding. I found this out when my daughter Denise was giving birth to her third child, and I was going to be her coach. She started labor, and off we headed to the hospital. They took her inside, and directed me to another room.

"Are you a medium?" a nurse asked me.

"No, I'm a guru." Just because I had a dot on my forehead and just because I wore a big pendant with the Sanskrit symbol for *Om*, that didn't make me some kind of fortune teller. If she wanted her tea leaves read, she'd better go someplace else.

"Well, you look like a medium to me."

Wow, this woman had some nerve, and so I started to spiel about the difference between being on a spiritual path and taking a side trip through the psychic worlds. She looked at me kind of strange. "Medium?" she said again. That's when I noticed she was holding up a nurse's scrub outfit. "Small, medium, or large?" All she wanted was for me to put on a gown and mask before I went into the delivery room.

LISTENING

Wisdom comes from listening to the soul.

How well do you listen to people? Do you care about other people enough to let them speak their minds?

You will notice that when you are listening to others, they are also listening to you. You can gradually learn to listen more and speak less, and bit by bit you will forget your hunger to be proven right. There will be only sharing and the end of isolation.

If you cannot hear another person, how do you think you will hear the whisper of intuition? How will you hear your own soul? The ego itself invites you into this karmic space precisely because it does not want you to listen to any voice except its own.

Maybe someone has suggested a richer way for you to live. "Oh no," says the small ego, "I know what's best for me." This is the most fundamental illusion of the ego, but it's hard to get a grip on it because, in fact, you *do* know what's best for you, but only if you follow your own intuitive heart instead of the voice of the ego.

Listening to others and listening to your inner voice go together. When you can listen, you begin to leave the space of the desire to be right. Once you can hear your own heart, rather than the ego's words, it becomes easier to hear the hearts of others.

It takes practice to hear the voice of your higher Self, and meanwhile the ego will keep right on claiming to be right. Still, wherever you begin, you have started to weaken another set of karmic reactions.

Practices for Letting Go

Always insisting on being right is a habit, but all habits can be broken. Sometimes it takes conscious effort to replace an old habit with one that is more positive. These simple practices can help.

ACTION: YOU MIGHT BE RIGHT

So what?

If you always consider that you might be wrong and the other person might be right, you will rarely hurt anyone; therefore you won't hurt yourself. The next time you feel you are being attacked, or the next time your cherished beliefs are being challenged, just say, "You might be right."

Make this a habit, before you put up your defenses. It's another form of the hesitation or non-reaction that loosens karma.

If you have the humility to do this, conflicts can end, and you can enter a place of spiritual maturity. You will still state your opinion, but you will remember that you never need to close your heart to another person.

BREATH: SPLIT THE TENSION

You hold pockets of stale karma in your body.

Tension can be felt throughout the body when one desperately wants to be right. Tightness interferes with the natural flow of shakti. To break up the blocks, I teach a meditation about "splitting the tension."

Sit quietly, with a straight back. Visualize the breath flowing horizontally in and out in each chakra, starting with the chakra at the base of the spine, and then moving up the chakras to the top of the head. The chakras control the free flow of energy, so pay attention to which chakra feels clogged with tension.

Now focus on the place where you feel the most tightness. Breathe in horizontally and breathe out as an upward flow, as if you are breathing through a straw in the center of the body that exits out the top of your head. As you breathe out, inwardly say, "Split the tension, split the tension." This is an easy natural breath. Do not strain.

This literally breaks up the tension into its smaller pieces, allowing you to let go of some of them. You can do this until you have very little tension, and what's left is just calmness.

CHAPTER THIRTEEN

Attachment

Recognizing the Karmic Space

No attachments, no karma.

Picture the karmic spaces like a row of cubbyholes with you stuck inside. Now imagine the karmic spaces filling with the warm waters of love and understanding. As your being is flooded, your soul can swim free. But there is a part of you that is still held fast, a small crab-like creature clinging to its cubbyhole, its hands and feet braced hard against the sides, gripping tight as the flood rises. This is attachment, or the attached ego, and it fights against your freedom.

I wrote earlier about attachment to worldly desires, but the deep karma of attachment is much bigger than that. We are attached to our possessions, our families, our thoughts, our emotions, our bodies, and even to our ideas of God. Yet the main thing we cling to is our small ego and its dramas. The karmic space of attachment is the master cubbyhole, all the karmic spaces rolled into one.

It is difficult for us to recognize this karmic space because we constantly confuse love and attachment. We also confuse personal power with attachment, because attachment lets us think we are in control, forgetting that we are just passing through this life and through the lives of others. Everything changes, and loss comes to all of us, but the more we hold on, the greater will be the pain of loss. When you let go of attachment, or when you begin to realize your essential Self, pettiness falls away and leaves you free to love and free to live.

You go through life either consuming the world or being consumed by it. If you are attached, then whatever happens in life takes up all the space in your heart and mind. This is how attachment eats up your life, or consumes it. When you learn to consume life, you take control of your own heart and your own mind, even in the chaos of life. You learn to use any experience, negative or positive, as fuel for your journey. As you learn to consume the world, you begin to experience your life more fully, you learn to grow from your experiences, and most important, you discover you can let go. Once you can consume this world, you are free.

ATTACHMENT TO EMOTION

There is no emotion in the chidakash, only pure love.

We can recognize the karmic space of attachment whenever we find ourselves caught in some kind of emotional drama. Like thoughts, emotions come and go; they have no roots unless we plant them. Deep-rooted emotional habits become *samskaras*, the building blocks of karma.

We can become attached to any emotion, including a painful one, if it makes us feel alive. We cling to emotion because we fear emptiness, and we fear emptiness because we imagine it to be somehow negative. The ego cries out, "Dwell here, don't look up, for here you will be much more comfortable." Yes, you certainly will be, because we are all used to being in our patterns of emotion. That's why we go into the karmic spaces in the first place, those dark cubby holes, so cozy and inviting.

Attachment to our emotions often feels hot and intense. By contrast, detachment feels cool, and so we mistake it for the coldness of indifference. Or, missing our dramas, we can mistake detachment for boredom.

But isn't love an emotion?

We have two hearts, which is another way of saying we experience love in two distinct ways. There is the emotional heart that we feel in the center of the chest, and there is the heart space over the head, which my teacher Swami Nityananda called the *chidakash*. If you breathe very gently, very quietly, into your chest and visualize that breath rising up through your body to a space just over the head, your awareness can reach the vastness of the *chidakash*, the sky of consciousness. Here, even in the midst of chaos, you can place your awareness on the breath coming in and going out, and you will find yourself becoming detached. Yet, at the same time you will remain caring. In the chapter on the karmic space of indifference, I explained how awareness of the *chidakash* helps prevent burnout when you are confronted with pain. However, detachment is much more than just a practical tool. It can become a way of life.

All emotion works the same way: Instead of looking up for a higher awareness, you spread out more and more in a horizontal way. If you're angry, if you're depressed, if you have made a habit of emotion, you may think that the state you're in is everlasting, as indeed it is if it keeps you caught in one of the karmic spaces. Instead of focusing on your emotions, think for a moment of the emptiness of the sky. The higher mind, the sky mind, is always there in everyone, a very clear space beyond the clouds.

When Swami Nityananda was first trying to teach me about the *chidakash*, I just didn't see how I could be detached from my husband and my children, or even why I would want to be. Then I had a vision: I saw myself walking into my children's bedrooms, one after another, and on each bed was just a little pile of ash. I freaked out, totally. These were my babies! I heard Swami's voice, "This is one hundred years from now." I understood, and even as I screamed and cried I saw the futility of attachment, even to the ones I loved the most.

Karmic Connections

Can you hold water in your hand, and will it still flow fresh and free? Can you love your children by crushing the life out of them? Can you possess the divine by clinging tight to it?

The answer to all of these is no. Yet we keep trying to do the impossible. We try to possess people and things, we court the disappointment of expectation, and we become seduced by psychic ability.

POSSESSION

Attached love is not love at all, it is possession.

In relationships and in families, attachment can replace love with possessiveness. Then attachment takes positive feelings and turns them into a destructive force.

We have all heard of women who were abused when they tried to leave a relationship, or parents who hurt their children rather than lose them. These are extreme cases, but most of us have hurt someone because of attachment. You may have allowed another person to become dependent on you, or maybe you were the one who gave up your freedom because you wanted someone to run your life. Have you used "I have a broken heart" as an excuse to turn to drink or drugs or any other self-destructive behavior? Or have you smothered your children in the name of protecting them? We're so used to all this that we hardly notice it, we just assume it's "human nature" and write songs and psychology books about it. But what does all this pain have to do with love?

In trying to possess our children, we forget that they are only loaned to us; we don't own them. Our children's souls have exactly the same perfection as our grown-up souls, and when we remember this we realize they weren't born just to take over the family business or do whatever we as parents think they should do. If you clutch tight to a child, you will lose that child. Give that child love and let him go, let him make his own mistakes, and that bond is forged forever.

Yet many mothers have told me, "What causes me the greatest amount of love also causes the greatest amount of pain, especially my relationship with my children." Attachment mixes itself into love, and the result is the deepest pain imaginable. I am a mother, and I understand this, completely. It is mothers who feel a child's pain as if it were their own, and it is mothers who are on guard every moment of every day to protect their children. This is the essence of compassion, the ability to feel what another person feels, and it comes easier to women because of a powerful combination of biology, culture, and experience. Many women have a harder time learning detachment than men, and many men have a harder time learning compassion. But we need not pay too much attention to cultural stereotypes of how men should be and how women should be, since we are all both masculine and feminine, with just differences in degree. In fact, a woman who has learned detachment actually becomes more powerful because she had so much more to work through, or so much fuel to burn as she learned the difficult art of love without attachment. Likewise, a man who has acknowledged his own compassionate nature finds new strength.

People who believe in reincarnation always want to know, "Was I with this lover in another life? Did he hurt me then too?" Or, "What is my karma with my family?" Or, after giving birth, a mother might ask, "Who *is* this baby, really?" These questions easily give way to attachment, so don't get so caught up in them. Instead ask:

How will I keep my heart open?

How can I learn to love unconditionally?

Am I hurting this person, and how can I stop?

Am I hurting myself, and how can I change?

These are the same questions that can guide any relationship, with or without believing in other lifetimes, and the answer is the same: Love everyone you meet, as best you can. So, to the question, "Who is this baby, really?" the answer is just, "He's somebody who needs you to take good care of him." The answer to "Did my husband hurt me last life?" becomes "Maybe, but so what?"

A STUDENT'S STORY: HEART OF GOLD

When I met my husband, it was love at first sight. I felt we were soul mates, and we entered a beautiful, joyful relationship. Sometimes, though, I noticed a different side, as if there was a darkness in him, or I saw how he could get nasty if anyone disagreed with him. But, most of the time, I was so in love I didn't see it or didn't care.

Seven months into our relationship we got married. About a year later, he pretty much just up and left, with no warning, and moved back to his old home in a different state. Until that day I was still in love with him. We were planning to have children and everything.

At first it was devastating, and I would have welcomed him back. But we were still in touch by phone and he was being really mean. Instead of feeling bad for myself—divorced, mid-thirties, abandoned, alone—suddenly I got angry. Anyone who knows me would say I am not an angry person, but I didn't like feeling like a victim. So all of a sudden, in the middle of a conversation, I realized, Who needs him? And I just hung up the phone.

It took a while, but after that I picked myself up and kept going, one step at a time. I had found this place inside me that was just untouchable. I knew it was my heart, this rock solid place inside me, which no one could hurt. He kept trying for a while, poking at me to see if he could get to me. By then I knew

(continues)

I was strong enough for anything, because literally I had a heart of gold. No one could touch that. Love is inside me, and he didn't take that away when he left. I began to see in myself a new stillness and conviction that I hadn't experienced before. Then I remembered the big picture, how much I loved God and that God was in control of my life. So I let go of this man that I had thought was going to be my whole world. Once I made up my mind, it wasn't so hard after all.

EXPECTATION AND DISAPPOINTMENT

Attachment is the steel band
that encircles all your other karmas.

Because we fear the unknown, we sometimes make the mistake of thinking our attachments put us in control. But attachment actually lessens our control over our lives. When our expectations don't work out, we get upset and allow our egos and emotions to sweep us away.

When you are not attached to outcomes in the form of expectations, you will not be surprised or hurt when things don't go your way. Detaching from our desired outcomes or expectations is the best approach to both success and failure. Think for a moment of a big goal, like finding a cure for cancer. Many people have spent their whole lives on this quest, often pursuing research that ended in nothing. Are their lives failures? No, because nothing is wasted in the universe. It is attachment to success that makes someone deeply unhappy over not attaining a goal. The work will be of use somehow, even if someone else gets the credit. Even if it has reached a complete dead end, the attempt offered a life with purpose. Failure is only another idea that arises from attachment.

Outside the karmic spaces is only joy, but that means the joy in doing what you're doing right now, not some future joy that begins only when you succeed. You tell yourself, I will be happy after I lose fifty pounds. I will be happy after I make my first million dollars. The fact is, if you're not happy now you won't necessarily be happy then. If you know this, you can do everything possible to reach your goal, and yet stay unattached to the outcome.

We get attached to our desire for praise and fear of blame. There is a saying attributed to the Buddha: "Just as a rock is not moved by the wind, so the wise man is not moved by blame or praise." This is true, but most of us are not that wise yet. Instead, I think of what a woman in India told me, "Just walk on like the elephant, and let the little dogs bark at your feet." Praise and blame certainly don't feel the same, no matter what the scriptures may tell us, but keep walking anyway. When either praise or blame has the power to stop you, that's when you are giving in to attachment.

THE PSYCHIC TRAP

Without awareness, the path is not a path at all;
it is just the ego's journey.

Ego hijacks spirituality in many ways, some of which I have mentioned, including spiritual pride and righteousness. We can get attached to certain states of consciousness that become more available to us as we begin to quiet our minds.

One of these is psychic ability, which can be enormously seductive. Visions. Colors. Past lives. Mind reading. Angels. Demons. I have seen people caught up in the psychic realm for years, in fact even for lifetimes. Without getting into a big discussion, I will say that, yes, these things are real, but they don't matter all that much. If they are beautiful, enjoy them and move on, like leaving the theater after a great movie. If they are frightening, then I will share with you something I learned when spiritual life was very new and confusing to me: Point at the vision, actually point with your finger, and ask firmly, "In the name of Christ, who are you?" (That's what I was taught, but you can say "In the name of love," if you'd rather.) If there is something hanging around you that is making you uncomfortable, it will vanish like a puff of smoke.

There is also attachment to bliss itself. Through meditation and other practices, we can reach states of calm and joy that we naturally want to hang on to, like anything else that feels good. When I taught in New York, sometimes I would lead a group of students into a guided meditation, and when they were getting too serious, suddenly I'd say, "Let's go to Carvel!" That was the ice cream shop right around the corner.

If you lead meditations you can't let yourself go too deep, just in case someone needs help, so you just sit there and keep watch. While everybody else in the room was thinking about God, I had been thinking about chocolate. But for anyone in deep meditation, it's quite jarring to have to return so suddenly to the ordinary world. I would watch to see who got angry, who couldn't get grounded enough to find their coats, and who pretended not to hear me. I really did want ice cream, but I also wanted to teach them to move easily between states of consciousness without attachment to any of them. It's not really all that hard to go into bliss; the hard part is bringing the bliss back into ordinary life.

You might even find that you become attached to the idea of not creating any karma or obsessed with not wanting to get stuck in the karmic spaces. You might also start to fear getting attached, which can be worse than attachment itself, because you'll always be analyzing and thinking about it instead of trusting your intuition. How can you enjoy anything in the moment if you are always worried about getting attached?

Eventually you will learn to live in many different states of awareness, but be attached to none. This is living in the moment.

Karmic Graces

No matter how we try to cling, the world is constantly changing. This is not a new thought. It's what Heraclitus meant when he said we can't step in the same river twice, and it's what the Buddha meant when he told his monks "All is burning." Since we can't control the world, we must look inside for ways to change our awareness. The surprising discovery is that, as you gradually let go of your patterns of attachment, you will find you don't miss them at all. Learning to love unconditionally and making a commitment to your soul will help you break the habit of attachment.

UNCONDITIONAL LOVE

Attachments fill up the spaces in you that could hold love.

The opposite of attachment is unconditional love. This is when you can say, I will love this person whether she loves me or not. This is incredibly freeing. You don't have to keep looking behind you.

Expecting to be treated decently in a relationship is not putting conditions on love, it's just common sense. That's why unconditional love has nothing to do with being a victim, although some people are confused about this. If your spouse or partner is abusing you, it's not a measure of love to put up with it, it's just a measure of attachment. Don't let "love" blind you, because that's not love at all. My guru told me, "Never throw anyone out of your heart." Still, there may be times when you have to throw someone out of your house.

It's easy to say "I love you," but then do you wait to hear "I love you" back? What happens inside if you don't hear it? If you wait for an echo, you are putting conditions on your love. Now you are attached to a certain outcome. Unconditional love never needs to be answered.

I tell my students, "Give and don't look to see who's taking." This is not easy, but it's something you can learn. In the early days of the AIDS epidemic, I would sit for hours in a little room in West Hollywood, and the whole day would pass with waves of the dying coming in and going out. When I first met these young men and women who were living with AIDS, they'd be full of life, and a few months later they'd be dying, sometimes literally in my arms. I had to fight every second not to be attached, because otherwise I would have been no help. We cried at times, but we laughed more.

At the same time, I couldn't bear to forget a single one, and I would keep all their pictures in little books that I carried around with me. That might not sound very detached, but detachment is not the same as coldness. I took those books with me and showed them to religious leaders as I begged them to bring more compassion to people with AIDS. Some heard, some didn't, but detachment kept me going. I could be with the dying, and I could speak to powerful people, all without pride or shame, because I finally understood the meaning of the *chidakash*, which is detachment and love flowing together.

COMMITMENT TO THE SOUL

Awareness of the soul is not a religion;
it is a state of consciousness.

Death is the greatest teacher because it shows the futility of all attachment. Do you truly think you own your body? You know better, if you have ever been to a funeral and heard those magnificent words, "Ashes to ashes, dust to dust." There is only one thing that is certain in this life, and that is the soul. All else changes, all else flows, but to seek the very substance that your soul is made of is to seek eternal life.

The attachment to your own higher Self eliminates all other attachments. This is because all else pales in comparison to it. Two objects cannot be in the same place fully at the same time. One takes more room or one pushes the other out. But how do you make a commitment to your soul?

Just by wanting to. That means giving up things you don't need, one by one, bit by bit—a pattern of anger, an attachment to someone, a habit of negativity. What's left is the soul, and the soul's joy. That's what this whole book really is, an instruction manual to help you find your soul. The details are different for each person, because we have different patterns of attachment, different karma, but the broad outlines are clear.

It may have been Jung who said, "The soul does not live in us, we live in the soul." If you think the soul lives in you, you make it small. If you live in the soul, you understand that it's universal, it's huge, it's always there, and you can feel it, beyond all pain, all sickness, all emotion, all attachment, everything.

Practices for Letting Go

All meditation and spiritual practice can help you grow in the awareness of your true Self. To loosen attachment, simply notice the flow of your breath. This brings you to a constant flow of awareness.

BREATH: THE FLOWING RIVER

Attachment is yesterday and tomorrow,
detachment is now.

All rivers lead to the ocean, and every soul will return to the universal soul. Yet, when you swim against the current, you can drown. When you cling tight to anything, not only does the river flow on without you, but the current tears at you. When you flow with the current, but with your own stroke, then you are conquering the current. This is the flow of awareness, and the flow of life itself.

This breath reminds us of the eternal flow of life and death, in the flow of the river. Close your eyes and feel your heart. Notice the deep silence surrounding you, especially the silence of the out breath.

Start by breathing in for a count of three.

Hold the breath for a count of six.

Slowly release the breath while you count to six.

And hold the breath out while you count to six.

Repeat this for four or five cycles at first. Gradually you can build up the number of cycles, and you can increase the count, but always keep the pattern of doubling the length of the in breath. If you are comfortable breathing in 4, do all the other steps to a count of 8, and so on.

After doing the breath, let yourself go into the silence, feeling the in breath flow into the out breath as life flows into death and back again.

PRAYER: DETACHED PRAYER

Attachment says, "Give me what I want."
Detachment says, "Thank you."

Sometimes we pray with great passion and emotion, until prayer and attachment mix together. For example if your child is sick, your prayer is very passionate, but it's possessive too. "*My* child," you say.

If you can learn to pray without attachment, the small self gets out of the way. You can learn not to be attached to the results of prayer, not to put time limits on when prayers are answered, and not to assume to know exactly how they should be answered.

To practice this, find three smooth stones. Holding the first stone, say a prayer for your child. Now hold the second stone and pray for someone else who is sick. Finally, with the third stone in your hand pray for someone else in need. Three similar prayers, for three people you care about, although you really just want to pray for your own child, because he's *yours*.

Close your hand, and move the three stones around like prayer beads in your hand. Soon you won't know which stone represents which person, so you pray for all three the same. Now your prayer flows clear, like spring water.

MEDITATION: WHO AM I

When giving up even the smallest attachment,
you are giving up a small piece of illusion.

Socrates said, "Know thyself." Jesus said, "The kingdom of God in within you." Ramana Maharshi used the same thought, based on the Vedas, as the core of his teaching. He taught us to ask again and again the great question: Who am I?

Sit quietly, and ask yourself that simple question, over and over. Who am I? When you begin this practice, your ego mind will offer you a whole list: "I am a mother," "I am a spiritual seeker," or even "I am depressed and lonely." Do not accept these labels. Recognize them as what they are—a list of your attachments.

Just keep going, and the question will reveal more and more. "I am God. I am love. I don't belong in these karmic cubbyholes." "I am the soul, and I don't have to be attached to anything."

This is a practice you can continue and deepen every day of your life. It is also a way to unstick yourself from anything that grabs you from one day to the next. The true answers are the ultimate ecstasy. But don't take my word for it, just start asking the greatest question.

MANTRA: OM

Attachment is the slayer of the soul;
detachment is the perfection of the soul.

Just as attachment holds you in all of the karmic spaces, the great universal sound of *Om* is a mantra that can free you from any of the cubbies. In eastern traditions, *Om* is considered to be the sound of the universe. It can be pronounced *"Om"* or *"Aum,"* but as you say it, use the whole out breath to draw out the sound. As you chant *Om*, the sound of this universal vibration enters inside you, opens the chest, and lifts you out of any kind of attachment. Your heart space automatically opens up.

So when thoughts invade your space during the day, nagging you over and over, say the sound of *Om*. You can chant *Om* out loud, or you can do it as a silent mantra. Something within you, your inner wisdom, will begin to awaken. And as you grow, the knots within you—physical, spiritual, and karmic knots—will begin to loosen.

PART THREE

Beyond The
Karmic Spaces

CHAPTER FOURTEEN

Freedom

Recognizing all the Karmic Spaces

*Light the candle of your awareness
and lead yourself out of negativity.*

T he karmic spaces represent life and death. You can choose
to live in your heart, or you can let yourself die a little bit
at a time, stuck inside the karmic spaces. When you feel
yourself slipping into darkness, remember that with awareness
you can find your way out of any karma.

Once you have been touched by even some understanding of
the karmic spaces, your awareness will expand step by step. Whenever you are stuck in the pain that the ego's thoughts bring to
your mind, you can pick up the tools of awareness, transcend the
ego's labels, and get out. You always have choice, and after every
choice, there is always another choice and another chance. Yet you
may wonder, Another chance at what? Where does this journey
lead me? That's up to you. You can use what you have learned to
go as far as you want.

Darkness is nothing more than the absence of light, and in
every space, no matter how dark, there is a tiny bit of light. Good
can always come from a bad space, even a terrible space, if you're
aware enough to look for it. Not only does awareness let you turn
and walk out of every karmic space, but it teaches you how to
pick up the light that will show you the way. These lights are what
I have been calling the karmic graces. Light is powerful—just consider what happens when you light a single match in a dark room.
The same thing happens when you bring a tiny spark of awareness

into the darkness of karma. You begin to know that you are capable of pouring light over yourself and others.

Recognizing the karmic spaces can bring joy back to your life, without the burdens of boredom and bad habits. Breaking apart the deadness of karma can help you get in touch with your body, your intuition, and your capacity to love.

If you choose to go further and follow the karmic spaces as a spiritual path, you can change your life, radically. Spirituality is not just a philosophy. It is a way of life. The cubbyhole teachings can bring freedom from the karma of lifetimes and can lead you to liberation. By this I mean what is taught in mystical traditions: to reach the source of eternity; to become that which we all seek, whether we know it or not; to find what we have sought through lifetimes, through anger, through pain, through jealousy, through pride, through every inch, every crack, every crevice of every karmic space.

Karmic Connections: Slaying the Ego

The ego is just an interruption of the great journey toward the oneness.

In every chapter of this book I have described the workings of ego. Although for each person it is individual and unique, like karma itself, the essence of the ego is to keep you separate, to imprison you in your mind, and to trick you into repeating old patterns, heart and eyes closed, reacting to life instead of mastering it.

The ego's negativity has created traps for you to keep falling into, and those have become the karmic cubby holes. They are the spaces where you don't have to face reality, the places to hide from your own perfection.

When you allow the ego to have its way, you can wallow in negativity forever. You can spend your whole life, even lifetimes, with the same old patterns. You can die, come back, and find yourself right there with the same negativity all over again, lifetime after lifetime.

It is impossible to know the Self through the ego mind.

And so, you must slay the ego. This simply means that you become the master of it so that it no longer controls you. Just working at doing this will change your life in profound ways. It is true what so many spiritual traditions teach: To truly live, we must die to our old way of life and be reborn into a new one.

How do you master the ego and slay it? Not by punishing yourself. This is where so many people get it wrong, thinking spiritual life is a recipe for self-denial. You will finally kill the ego, not by hating it, but by loving it. The ego cannot live in love. The ego is not separate from you, and in fact nothing is separate in you, which means you're going to have to love yourself.

This is the hardest thing you will ever do.

Karmic Graces

I have described specific qualities like gratitude and humility as graces that can lead us out of the karmic spaces, but in reality grace is bigger than any one quality, just the same as ego is too big to fit into any one karmic space. Grace takes many forms. There's the grace of your own increasing awareness. And there's the grace that comes to you through a spiritual teacher. In the end, grace is whatever allows you to choose freedom from karma—*in this life*. It beckons you as a light, revealing itself as you clear away the dark corners of the karmic spaces.

ACCUMULATED AWARENESS

Fate is when you don't pay attention.

We can visit a karmic space again and again, but at the same time we also revisit the wisdom or the awareness that we may have already found in that space. With even that small amount of awareness, we learn to turn around and walk out of any space. Don't expect to grasp it all at once, but each time you open the doors of awareness, your higher mind gets stronger.

As you get to know the karmic spaces, you can follow your breath in and out of them with very deep awareness, blowing away the cobwebs. Now your memory is ignited and you intuitively begin to remember things you have done and to recognize patterns. Then, maybe next time, you will choose not to go there. Not again, you say, clearing that bit of karma away, and you go on, but you've started something—you're awakening things in you—and it becomes like an avalanche. The walls of karma begin collapsing all around you.

You have no control over what the ego tells you, but as you grow in awareness, you can pick and choose what to listen to. You can develop the habit of saying to yourself, It's just a thought, whether you say this in meditation or in the middle of your day. If you ignore the ego long enough, it just begins to wither and die.

Now try saying to yourself, I wonder what my next thought will be? Or, like the master of ceremonies at an awards show, Next? This is how you confuse the ego until it gets out of the way and lets you be. After a while, you'll be able to just hear the Self speak instead of the ego. You don't have to be completely out of the karmic spaces to understand the ecstasy that the journey can bring. You don't have to be "liberated" to feel a new birth of joy. When you're quiet enough to hear the Self, it becomes a joy, even if you still have pain in your life.

Maybe you're not ready, so you take a step back, or maybe you run all the way back into darkness. But awareness, once it begins, can only grow. Once you get a little taste of freedom, you will want more, and eventually all the karmic spaces are affected. One day you wake up, but you wake up dead to the ego.

Then you will know: I can take what I need, because it is mine; I can give away what I do not need because it is not mine.

Everything you need is available. It's your birthright just because you are human, but you don't need to cling to any of it. Once you deeply understand this, then you will be filled with a universal love that will fill your life with abundance.

THE HEART OF THE PATH

Grace comes to you through the heart of the path.

The ultimate reality is the formless and it is impersonal, the way light is impersonal, shining on everything equally.

Some seekers try to reach straight for pure awareness of the formless, which is like climbing up a very steep staircase with no handrails. For most of us, we need a guide, a teacher, or the form of a Beloved—someone who can open our hearts and teach us to love. For many of us in the West, that someone is the Christ who, through love, opens the path to the Father. In Indian traditions, divinity takes many forms, yet on every path love is always love.

The heart of the path is the teacher—whether in the form of a living teacher, or a spiritual tradition, or writings left by a teacher—it is one who has walked ahead but who has left you with a path to follow. That's one type of grace, that there is always someone who went before you and is turning around to show you the way. Without this guide you would not understand the path, but by opening your eyes with new awareness you will find one who leads you, beckons you, calls you. It could be a priest, preacher, rabbi, imam, swami, guru, master, shaman—the label doesn't matter. The teacher you follow has learned from someone else, and so it continues, the wheel goes around and around, and then all of a sudden you see a moment of truth. That's how you jump out of a karmic cubbyhole, like a shortcut. Sometimes that's how grace comes.

You can call grace to you, but you cannot find it for anyone else other than yourself. Honor all teachers, but find your own particular path so that the answers will fit the space of your heart.

YOU WITHOUT EGO

I looked for God and found myself.

The teacher and the path open you to grace, but where does it really come from?

Grace is the you that is beyond anything, beyond names, beyond words, beyond form. You *are* the perfection. Catching just a glimpse of this is grace, and awareness grants you grace. Grace is the moment of the deepest awareness you have ever had. You grant yourself grace by going past all the chattering of mind and ego to a place of light.

People run around looking for a soul mate, a person to love forever, even into death, a person to share everything with. There is no such person. The other Self you are seeking is not in the past or the future, it is not some other place in time or space, it is *you*. Your soul mate is yourself—you without ego. Since we exist in different dimensions at the same time, there really are two of you, light and dark, in the same moment. There is the "you" who listens to ego, and there is the "you" without ego, the Self you keep searching for.

When you look for God, you're really looking for yourself. That's very hard to accept because we've been taught that God is so far beyond us. Different religions and philosophies argue on and on about the exact connection between the human and the divine, but once you begin to experience divinity for yourself, these arguments become irrelevant. For this we have the words of the great scholar and philosopher Saint Thomas Aquinas who, after a mystical experience, said, "All that I have written seems to me like straw, compared to what has now been revealed to me."

So here we are, stranded for a while in this life, each with our tasks to do, big or small, yet each knowing that there must be more to life. You may pray to a personal God, or you may reject that idea and just focus on your own awareness, but either way the spiritual path will always lead you back to the Self. You are asking for your own grace that has been stored in the universe waiting for you to call it to you. You're asking for the grace that can come from your Self without ego—the same Self that will get you out of the karmic cubbyholes.

LIBERATION

Liberation is accessible to anyone who breathes.

When we think about liberation, most of us think of heaven instead of earth.

Yet liberation does not happen in the heavens at all; liberation happens here on earth to ordinary people who are not ordinary at all. There is a uniqueness about those who have reached the ultimate awareness, and yet they are just like everyone else.

Swami Nityananda always said, "You must return from whence you have come." He meant, don't wait for a bright light or anything else to guide you at death, because that light is available always. You have come from the light, you have come from perfection, and you will return there after death. That's not quite liberation, though—that's just what is. You're still subject to karma because you're not finished; there are still pieces to complete in your karmic puzzle.

Liberation is accessible to anyone who breathes. I mean that quite literally, liberation is available in life—this life. Right here is where you have the ability to go toward your own perfection. When you allow your Self to be fulfilled with your own beauty, then your heart will stay open no matter how hard the ego tries to keep it closed. You are not afraid any more. Even in the midst of life's pains, you are filled with joy.

A STUDENT'S STORY:
JUST YOUR HEART

Suddenly, as the music filled me, I felt at first a slow up-rushing of joy, and then to my astonishment a soft but violent explosion in the middle of my chest, to the right of my heart, and I was carried swiftly on the waves of the singing into an extraordinary ecstasy. Though I knew that this had been working in me for many years, still it took me so much by surprise that I fell to the floor, gasping and laughing and crying out. I had never felt anything remotely like it in my entire life—it was far more powerful than orgasm, deeper, softer, inexpressibly more joyful, a continuous and unabating happiness, a simple incandescence, a single blaze of immense, unsupportable happiness.

I went out onto the balcony and watched the gulls climbing, falling and gliding along the walls of the Palisades, above the bright expanse of the river. The wind carried them wherever they inclined, over the shining water, and in their movement I felt an amazing freedom, awareness, evenness, oneness, love.

Was it love exactly? Yes, and yet it seemed so impersonal. It just was. I went on a walk in the streets of Riverdale. Everyone I passed had the same love in his eyes, shining and ineffable. Everyone had it, in exactly the same measure. Behind all the masks, thick or thin, of anger or pride, sorrow or weariness, everyone was rejoicing. By some unintelligible grace, my heart had opened to the wonder and beauty of the world, and there was nothing left for me to do, for the rest of my life, but to burn with gratitude, from the depth of whatever thankfulness God gave me.

After my walk I called my teacher, Hilda Charleton. "What have you done to me?" By now, I was absurdly worried about my civil rights—no one had told me that this was real, that I might

(continues)

without my consent be suddenly transported out of the commonplace world. I was like a man furious at having been woken before the alarm went off.

"I haven't done a thing dear," Hilda said. "It's just your heart opening. Relax and enjoy it. And ignore yourself." She laughed and hung up. When I put the phone down, I realized I had simply got what I had asked for, what I had sought since childhood, and nothing less.

Follow Your Grace

You could change your destiny every single second.

Joseph Campbell said "Follow your bliss," and I change that just a little to "Follow your grace." By following grace, you discover that the karmic spaces have become places of brightness in your life, so bright they can even hold ecstasy. To go into a karmic space that has been cleared out and purified is like going into a light that is so magnificent you feel it throughout your whole body. As you go into this pure light you actually say to yourself, This is what I missed.

To understand this, look back to the first karmic cubbyhole, jealousy. It's still the space of jealousy, but now it's also the space of self-love and gratitude, which are the karmic graces that help you the most when jealousy entangles you.

It's not that the karmic spaces dissolved, it's that they've been full of light the whole time and you didn't know it. At first you saw just that tiny speck of light, and now the whole space is light with just a tiny speck of darkness. Grace was always there.

Why a speck of darkness? You need to remember so you can explain it to others. You can't hold on to this grace, because attachment closes down awareness, and lack of awareness closes down grace. So in the end, you have to share it. The wheel turns a little more.

Now What?

*Divinity is in the ordinary moment
that you live with awareness.*

One day, when all that illusion is gone, when there's nothing but pure bliss, you have to learn what to do with this much power.

I often say to my students that I looked for God and found myself. That's exactly what happened. But don't for a moment think I didn't fight it. I yearned, I prayed, I begged, I sought God with everything in me, and at the exact same time I fought against it. In my case, I held on to my tough Brooklyn street-kid pride. I sought God, but I didn't want to surrender.

In my daily life I had tasted every joy known to womanhood. I was complete, I was happy. But from the very second that the Christ appeared to me, I knew I had no joy whatsoever. There was no comparison, it was worlds and worlds and worlds apart.

The joy of God can fill you, can erase all sorrows, can replace all earthly joys. It eases, it protects, it fulfills.

And though the fear was so great, once I knew the joy of God, nothing earthly remained the same. Then I had to learn again to live, because I knew that God must be shared. But this is not India, and you can't run around in a state of God intoxication saying you met yourself and you are really God.

Well, actually, I tried that for a little while, since I thought my vision of Christ meant "Teach always," although what he really said was, "Teach *all* ways." So I got out my soapbox and started in on the Italian housewives of Brooklyn. Some thought I was crazy, some thought I was blasphemous, and some just didn't really want to hear about it.

So freedom is not quite what you might expect. Everything is colored differently, nothing is the same. It's all different, and it's all brighter. You discover you are fully human and fully divine in the same moment. You discover that you can have ecstasy and the earth, God and the world, all at once.

Now the journey really starts. You have great wisdom, but you still have to take out the trash. It's not just about service. It's not even just about God. It's about knowing your beauty. We've been told before, "You are made in the image of God." Can you accept that? Can you let it happen to you?

That's what this whole book is about. Let it be. Just let it be. Don't fight your own beautiful spirit.

The ego has one think that there are mysterious karmas.

There is no mystery to karma.

One breathes and one lives.

One breathes and one loves.

One breathes and one serves.

One simply breathes.

ACKNOWLEDGMENTS

I am forever grateful to my Guru, Neem Karoli Baba, and my teacher, Swami Bhagawan Nityananda, whose teachings have remained with me always, perhaps lifetimes.

My deep gratitude goes to everyone who worked so diligently on this book as well as to my students and my family, who have supported me since the beginning of my journey.

I offer many thanks to Kashi Ashram, which holds and sustains me every day and whose beauty is beyond words.

I also thank all teachers of spirituality and all those who serve and care for humanity.

And, finally, my pranams and love go to my dear friend Yogi Bhajan.

ABOUT THE AUTHOR

Born into a Jewish family in 1940, Ma Jaya Sati Bhagavati grew up in a cellar apartment in Brighton Beach, Brooklyn, just a short walk from the ocean and the famous Coney Island Boardwalk. As a young girl, she found love and solace among the homeless people who lived under the Boardwalk. Welcoming her, they taught her many lessons about life, especially, "There are no throwaway people." She grew up to dedicate her life to humanity.

Enrolling in a weight loss class in 1972 led her to learn a simple yogic breath that would ultimately bring about her spiritual enlightenment. Her personal spiritual journey moved quickly and at times chaotically. As a thoroughly modern urban woman, she tried to live a normal life and raise a family; at the same time, as a person of rare spiritual gifts, she daily opened to a series of mystical visions and experiences. She had an experience first of Jesus Christ, then of Shri Bhagawan Nityananda of Ganeshpuri, and finally her guru, Shri Neem Karoli Baba. As early as 1973, she began to "teach all ways," giving a contemporary voice to the great truths that underlie all spiritual paths.

In 1976, Ma Jaya moved to Florida and founded Kashi Ashram, a spiritual community that embraces all religious and spiritual paths, where she continues to teach and serve. She became known for her passionate interfaith advocacy of people living with HIV/AIDS, and for her support of the LGBT community. Among her other accomplishments are developing Kali Natha Yoga, a modern yoga system drawn from ancient roots; guiding the River Fund, a service organization with projects in India, Uganda, and the United States; founding By the River, a model community for low income seniors; and creating a large body of sacred art.

Ma Jaya is considered by many to be a spiritual master who has attained inner realization. She teaches that divinity is ultimately beyond words and without form, yet manifests in countless ways to lead us to liberation. She embraces an interfaith approach, believing that all paths of love lead to the truth. She offers the example of a spiritual life alive with love, faith, creativity, service, and the rituals of many traditions. Emphasizing individual spiritual growth, she teaches seekers at all levels and does not ask her students to follow any particular set of doctrines or beliefs. Or, as Ma Jaya puts it when she describes her own teachings, "This is not a religion!" Rather, she encourages her students to use what she teaches within their own faiths or traditions. She asks them only to practice kindness.

For more information about Ma Jaya and her teachings, visit the Kashi Ashram website at www.kashi.org. You can learn more about the 11 Karmic Spaces at www.karmicspaces.com.

CPSIA information can be obtained at www.ICGtesting.com
Printed in the USA
LVOW01s0426260713

344719LV00009B/425/P